PRINCIPLES OF QUANTITATIVE EQUITY INVESTING

Principles of Quantitative Equity Investing

A Complete Guide to Creating, Evaluating, and Implementing Trading Strategies

Sugata Ray, PhD

Publisher: Paul Boger
Editor-in-Chief: Amy Neidlinger
Acquisitions Editor: Charlotte Maiorana
Operations Specialist: Jodi Kemper
Cover Designer: Chuti Prasertsith
Managing Editor: Kristy Hart
Senior Project Editor: Betsy Gratner
Copy Editor: Karen Annett
Proofreader: Jess DeGabriele
Indexer: Lisa Stumpf
Compositor: Nonie Ratcliff
Manufacturing Buyer: Dan Uhrig

This book is sold with the understanding that neither the author nor the publisher is engaged in rendering legal, accounting, or other professional services or advice by publishing this book. Each individual situation is unique. Thus, if legal or financial advice or other expert assistance is required in a specific situation, the services of a competent professional should be sought to ensure that the situation has been evaluated carefully and appropriately. The author and the publisher disclaim any liability, loss, or risk resulting directly or indirectly, from the use or application of any of the contents of this book.

For information about buying this title in bulk quantities, or for special sales opportunities (which may include electronic versions; custom cover designs; and content particular to your business, training goals, marketing focus, or branding interests), please contact our corporate sales department at corpsales@pearsoned.com or (800) 382-3419.

For government sales inquiries, please contact governmentsales@pearsoned.com.

For questions about sales outside the U.S., please contact international@pearsoned.com.

Company and product names mentioned herein are the trademarks or registered trademarks of their respective owners.

ISBN-10: 0-13-487845-0
ISBN-13: 978-0-13-487845-4

Pearson Education LTD.
Pearson Education Australia PTY, Limited.
Pearson Education Singapore, Pte. Ltd.
Pearson Education Asia, Ltd.
Pearson Education Canada, Ltd.
Pearson Educación de Mexico, S.A. de C.V.
Pearson Education—Japan
Pearson Education Malaysia, Pte. Ltd.

Library of Congress Control Number: 2015936653

To my family.

Contents

ACCESS COLOR FIGURES

If you would like to study the figures in this book more closely, color versions are available from the book's Web site, www.ftpress.com/title/9780134192796. Click the Downloads tab to access them.

Acknowledgments

I am grateful to editors Karen Annett, Betsy Gratner, and Charlotte Maiorana, and the rest of the team at Pearson for helping me through the daunting process of putting a book together. I am also grateful to Kate Fernandes and Jeanne Levine for helping this book find a home at Pearson. I am grateful to Vikas Agarwal, Deniz Anginer, John Banko, Anthony Canalungo, Alicia Cofino, Henry Crutcher, Emily Crutcher, Wes Gray, Kaitlyn Harrow, Paul Huebner, Phillip Hulme, Yan Lu, David Merahn, Mahendrarajah Nimalendran, and students in my FIN 4414 class in the fall of 2014 and spring of 2015 for suggestions and feedback. I would like to thank Kyle Cerminara, Lewis Johnson, and the rest of the team at Fundamental Global Investors and Capital Wealth Advisors for their thoughts on quantitative investing. I am particularly grateful to Henry Crutcher and David Merahn for helping me with some of the more troublesome sections of the book. I am (and we should all be) grateful to Equities Lab for providing an extended trial for book users. Finally, I am especially grateful to my wife, Shalini, for bearing with me and improving the piece in myriad ways.

About the Author

Sugata Ray teaches and conducts research at the University of Florida. Ray's research has been published in a number of peer-reviewed journals, including the *Journal of Investment Management* and the *Journal of Financial Markets*. Ray's work has been presented to regulators, including those at the SEC and the Fed; academics at conferences such as the American Finance Association and European Finance Association; and industry participants. Ray's research has been covered in CNN, *The Economist*, the *Financial Times*, NPR, and *The Wall Street Journal*, among numerous other trade and popular press outlets. In addition to his academic pursuits, Ray also develops and manages quantitative investment strategies for Fundamental Global Investors, an investment company, and Capital Wealth Advisors, a wealth management company. Previously, Ray worked in various capacities in a number of financial services firms and asset managers, including Legg Mason, Oliver Wyman, and Lehman Brothers. He received his Doctorate, Master's, and Bachelor's degrees from the Wharton School at the University of Pennsylvania. You can read more about the author at his website: www.sugata.in.

Preface

What This Book Is About (and Not About) and Who It Is For (and Not For)

This book is about investing in U.S. equities using quantitative strategies. It is not about investing in most other things. For example, it is not about investing in bonds, mutual funds, CDs, or real estate. It is not about investing in other countries.[1]

This book is not about *trading* U.S. equities. Although trading is a part of investing in U.S. equities, it is a small part. Strategies discussed in this book are largely of the buy-and-hold nature, with occasional trades in the portfolio. If you are looking for a book on trading in and out of stocks multiple times within a day (also called *day trading*), this book is not for you.

This book is for (1) investors with money to invest who are learning how to invest using quantitative techniques, (2) professional financial advisors who manage money for clients and are looking to introduce quantitative techniques in their management processes, and (3) students who are interested in learning quantitative investing.

This book is not for speculators or "investors" who buy stocks based on recent headlines. Most quantitative strategies pick no-name stocks and hold them for long periods of time (quarters or years). It's not as exciting as owning Facebook or Apple over an earnings announcement, but historically, this strategy has performed just fine.

Additionally, this book is tailored to the level of a lay audience. If you are interested in a book with advanced mathematical concepts applied to finance, this is probably not the book for you. Similarly, if you are a hard core coder, looking to apply your coding skills to the financial markets, this is probably not the book for you.

The tool used most often in this book is a piece of software called Equities Lab. All legal, new purchases of this book include a 20-week trial subscription to Equities Lab (see the "Getting an Equities Lab Account and Logging In" section in Chapter 2, "What You Need to Start Investing Using Quantitative Techniques," for details on how to download and install Equities Lab). The second most common tool used in this book is Microsoft Excel. Any spreadsheet software (including free ones, such as Google Docs) should work fine.

Throughout the book, screenshots and techniques are shown using Equities Lab and Excel. These are simple, easy-to-use software packages that can deliver commercial-level analysis. The hope is that you will be able to follow along by repeating the analysis shown in the book (and experimenting with screens of your own). Finally, if you are interested in moving on beyond Equities Lab (or if your trial subscription has ended), check out Chapter 15, "Alternative Tools for Quantitative Investing," which covers alternate tools you can use.

Concrete Scenarios of Readers Who Would Find This Book Useful

If you are convinced this is the right book for you and are ready to read on, I suggest you skip ahead to Chapter 1, "Overview of Quantitative Investing." If you are still debating whether this is the right book, I will outline a few concrete scenarios where this book may be helpful to make your decision easier. As a reader of this book, you likely fall into one of several categories, as follows:

- Investors with money to invest who are learning how to invest using quantitative techniques
- Professional financial advisors who manage money for clients and are looking to introduce quantitative techniques in their management processes
- Students who are interested in learning quantitative investing

The following sections cover a few more explicit scenarios and how this book could potentially work for each of these types of investors.

Individual Investors Who Are Relatively New to Investing

Perhaps you are a busy professional with no brokerage account. You have never bought stocks or participated in the financial markets outside of your 401k, where you've invested in the default option.

Before investing the time and effort into learning quantitative investing strategies, you should convince yourself that they are worth learning. The easiest way to do this is to run a small cap value screen, or any other screen that is known to work (see Chapter 10, "Some Powerful Screens"), and write down the results. Make a list of the stocks the screen picks that the model suggests should outperform the market. While you track the progress of the picks to see if they do truly outperform, learn about investing in general (and read this book). If the stocks you picked using the screen did beat the market handily over a month or so (as they are statistically likely to do), you might be hooked and ready to take the plunge into quantitative investing in earnest.[2] When ready, deposit a small amount of money into a brokerage account (you really must be able to lose this money, or it will add too much stress to your life), and consider yourself a busy professional with a brokerage account (that is, the investor described later).

Individual Investors Who Have Invested in Equities Before But Are Not Professionals or Semiprofessionals at Investing

This category covers a large number of readers. You are likely to have had a bit of experience investing in equities directly and have an online brokerage already set up. The key here is experimenting with quantitative techniques, learning with small amounts of money, and growing that amount as your confidence increases.

You could start by paper trading: not trading for real money but keeping track of what "buys" and "sells" are suggested by your chosen quantitative trading model and simulating a profit and loss statement using those trades. However, you should be sure to switch over to a real money account at some point. You don't need to have 50 positions in quantitative strategies right off the bat; a small handful is fine as a start. You can't learn how to manage risk until you take some. By the same token, stick to money you can easily afford to lose. You are extremely unlikely to lose it all, but keeping the amount small prevents the roller-coaster ride of emotions that can make it hard to think. If you're stressed about it while at work, you need to worry less or reduce the amount you have invested.

You'll want to pick a couple of screens that have performed well historically and suit your investment style. Pick a few stocks from the screen output to invest in, and now you're a quantitative investor. Your first few tries might be somewhat rocky. This book will hopefully help you avoid some of the more obvious mistakes, but many less obvious ones remain. But as they say, practice makes perfect—and there is no substitute for learning by doing.

Involuntary Investors Who Receive a Cash Windfall

You've just inherited money, earned a massive bonus at work, or otherwise come into a lot of money. You've never invested before and have no idea what you're doing. The first thing you should do is probably consult a broader resource on investing in general. The next thing you should do is invest in index funds (S&P 500 or some other index) with your money. This will prevent you from missing out on market returns while you figure out what to do.[3] You will gradually sell these index funds as you develop strategies, but tracking the market will put you ahead of 80% of the people out there. This type of investment is tax efficient, easy, and good enough to start with.

Having done this, start with one of the other scenarios (perhaps "Individual Investors Who Are Relatively New to Investing"), and begin investing. Investing well will make your nest egg last a lot longer than investing poorly, and developing good investing habits right off the bat will go a long way toward your prosperity. One thing to keep in mind is that you'll be a bit more risk averse than others, at least to start with, because unlike investors investing money saved up from a salary, you most likely can't reproduce the circumstances that caused the windfall.

That's OK. As you learn more, you'll become comfortable taking on more risk. Because you didn't have the money before the windfall event, you obviously aren't dependent on it. This should help reduce your stress. Also, depending on the sum of the windfall, consider hiring a CPA and other advisors to help you with your affairs and taxes, at least for a year or two. There are a number of ways to optimize taxes and financial setups for windfalls, and doing things right from the start could save a lot of money and headache later on.

Investors and Investment Advisors Who Invest Mainly in Mutual Funds and ETFs

There are likely to be both investors and financial advisors who invest large chunks of their portfolios in funds. This has been the commonly dispensed advice by financial gurus: Invest in cheap passive index funds or exchange traded funds (ETFs). These investors are familiar with the mechanics of buying financial instruments through a brokerage, but have possibly never thought about individual stocks.

This book actually fits very well with this advice. The only difference is that rather than being constrained to the ETF/index funds out there, quantitative tools allow these investors to create a custom basket of securities that basically acts like a fund. Furthermore, many ETFs/index funds have holdings that don't accurately match up to their names. So while you might think that XYZ Bank's Value ETF actually holds value stocks, you might open the prospectus and examine the holdings and find value has been loosely defined to include speculative biotech companies!

Investors and Investment Advisors Who Invest in Individual Stock Picks

There are also investors and advisors among you who have invested in individual securities. Whether this is after doing a thorough valuation of a stock or after reading a couple of news articles, you are familiar with how to buy individual stocks. The main difference is that quantitative strategies will have you buying stocks based on different metrics than before. Instead of basing purchases off deep fundamental valuations, or meticulous reading of the news, quantitative strategies will use numbers reported by the company (and all other companies) to determine which stocks are most suitable for your portfolio.

To fit quantitative investing into your existing investment style, you'll want to use it as a source of ideas at first. Find a screen that gives you companies that you understand, and that performs well, and use it to find a new stock you like. Do your normal research on it, and invest in that stock as you normally would. Repeat the process several times in the coming weeks, and see how those stocks perform relative to your regular ones. If they outperform, consider automating more of your process. That is, cutting out the step of deep research into each of the names produced by the screen, and simply investing equally in all names produced by the screen. You can then spend the time saved refining the screen to make it perform better or creating other screens that capture other attributes you look for.

Investors and Investment Advisors Who Already Have a Quantitative Strategy in Place

If you already have a quantitative strategy in place, you've already implemented a system. You can make another one easily. Or improve the current one. Or test any assumptions you've made empirically; for example, are low price to earning (PE) ratio companies really good investments? If you test every testable assumption of your system, you may be shocked at what does (and doesn't) matter. You may find your strategy is really driven by one or two key criteria in your screens and the rest are not that useful.

Finally, a Note for Investors Who Have a Legacy Account

Maybe you have just inherited your grand aunt's stock portfolio. Maybe you've just bought an investment advisory business from a friend. Whatever the reason, you don't know what half of the things in your portfolio are.

Before embarking on any asset reallocation plans, the first question for you is how long ago were these positions bought, and what is their cost basis? If the cost basis is small, think really hard before selling. Make sure you have a better investment lined up. You'll pay significant taxes on gains if you sell, and that taxed money could have stayed in your account, compounding returns, if you held on to the position longer. If you believe you have positions that are going to underperform the market long term, you should go ahead and take your medicine, as directed by any tax advisor you might be using. Otherwise, just trim away at them by replacing them with better investments, until you have only the ones you like. One other consideration: If you have a concentrated position (for example, in tech), you'll need to adjust your strategies to not buy any more of that sector or industry. That way, you can use new money deployed to contribute toward diversification.

As with any cash windfall, strongly consider hiring a CPA for a couple of years after getting the brokerage account, as reconciling the cost basis of your positions is best done by a professional.

Student Scenarios

Finally, for students looking to learn about quantitative investing, a few words of wisdom from someone who was once in your shoes.

The Finance Student

You're a student, either in a finance course or business major, and want to see what quantitative investing is all about. Perhaps your professor has recommended or required this book for a class. You've got a bit of time and (probably) very little money to invest. This is no problem. However, you've actually got two problems to solve. One is learning how to invest, and the other one is determining if you like investing. If you end up deciding you like investing and you learn how to invest well (using quantitative techniques or otherwise), you potentially have a pretty lucrative career ahead of you.

Even if you don't end up choosing investing professionally as a career, you will always be tasked with investing your own money. As a student, your time horizon is at least 50 years (probably much longer), and your lack of money is not an issue at all. You can easily afford to lose what discretionary money you have (not including money used for tuition or rent) because you have high future labor income to replenish your savings. This gives you more risk tolerance than you will ever have in the future. You'll want to explore various strategies, and find screens that outperform. Try creating some basic screens. If you have a bit of disposable capital, implement screens that suit your temperament. The time you spend experimenting with the market will be well rewarded, as you'll find out what sorts of screens and systems you like, and whether you like investing at all. In addition, your lack of money is likely very temporary, so learning to invest now is a good idea. Very soon, you'll be joining the ranks of one of the investor categories described earlier. Trained in quantitative techniques, you'll be able to earn hefty returns on your newly earned capital.

The Technical Student

You are an engineering or computer science student interested in quantitative investing because you have heard tales of fabulous riches from financial investing. Maybe you're taking a course in the business school that covers quantitative investing. This book won't help you with your engineering coursework, but virtually everything else holds true from the previous "The Finance Student" section.

You might feel uncomfortable because you don't have a finance degree, but it might not occur to you that your other skills could be incredibly useful. For instance, people who can program or work in technical fields can often handle more complexity than those who do not. They may very likely find it easier to create screens that exactly describe what they are looking for.

Bon Voyage

As you dive into the rest of the book, and hopefully into the exciting and profitable world of quantitative investing, I wish you all the best and look forward to hearing about your exploits. Please feel free to send me war stories and comments about the book. You can e-mail me at sugata.ray@gmail.com. If you want to join an online community of quantitative investors and exchange information about quantitative investing techniques, Equities Lab maintains a forum at their website www.equitieslab.com.

Endnotes

1. That being said, a lot of the lessons from quantitative U.S. equity investing are applicable in these other contexts. If you have data for these other markets and can readily trade in them, you should feel free to start a quantitative investing agenda in your preferred market.

2. If the stocks picked by the screen did not outperform the market, then you may well lose interest, but it's probably worth trying again. Quantitative investing *does* work. Generally, over a month, it will probably work, but like any investing, aberrations occur, leading to underperformance in some fraction of months.

3. The overall market generally outperforms cash (or other risk-free, liquid investments) handily by about 6% a year. It is true that in a given day, week, month, or even year, the market may do worse, but over the long run, you are generally better off with your investable money in the stock market rather than in cash.

1

Overview of Quantitative Investing

Quantitative investing is generally defined as the use of a rigorous set of rules based on easily observable criteria to guide investment decisions. It encompasses a wide variety of strategies, from longer-term equity strategies where equities are bought and held for periods up to or longer than a year, to very short-term strategies trading in and out of securities multiple times during the course of a day. Of course, these shorter-term strategies do not really "invest" in the securities. Regardless of the exact type of strategy employed, there are several common steps in all types of quantitative investing: (1) screens, (2) backtests, and (3) implementation. This general process is graphically represented in Figure 1.1.

Screens

A screen is a formula for deciding what to buy and sell at any given time. A simple screen might be: Buy all stocks that have positive returns over the last year.[1] This is an example of a stock screen, which divides the universe of stocks into those the system will pick to buy and those it will not. A more complicated stock screen could have multiple criteria, such as "buy all stocks that have positive returns over the last year AND price to earnings (PE) ratios between 5 and 15."

As opposed to stock screens, you can also implement timing screens. *Timing screens* are screens that use some measure of the overall economy to decide whether it is a good time to buy or sell. An example of a timing screen could be "Move all assets to SPY if unemployment has fallen two months in a row. Otherwise, keep all assets in cash." SPY is the ticker for a security that mirrors the S&P 500 index. Thus, the screen basically keeps money in the broad equity markets if the economy is stable and in cash if unemployment is rising.

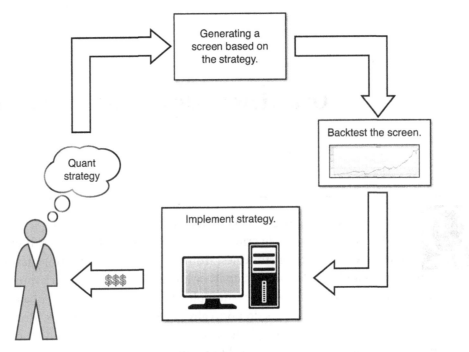

Figure 1.1 Life cycle of a quant investment

The difference between timing screens and stock screens can be subtle, and a number of screens will have flavors of both types. "Buy all stocks if unemployment has fallen two months in a row, and buy only stocks with PE ratios between 5 and 15 if not" is a screen that combines timing and stock screen elements. This book generally keeps them separate, but it is important to remember that they could be used together, if desired.

A screen generally returns a list of stocks and then a decision must be made. For example, the screen "Buy all tech stocks with PE ratios less than 10 that are profitable and pay a dividend" might return a list of about 15 stocks. The next step is to decide what to do with these lists. Generally, the easiest (and most popular) strategy among quantitative investors is to invest capital equally in all stocks that pass through a screen. So if 15 stocks pass through the screen, you divide the money you are investing equally into the 15 stocks and that will be your portfolio. There are other ways to weight the list: For example, you can weight by market capitalization or by dividends. Alternatively, you could do deeper fundamental analysis on the company names generated by the screen and pick individual securities to invest in, rather than simply dividing your capital equally among the companies that pass through the screens.

You should feel free to use screens to support deeper analysis of individual companies. Chapter 4, "For the Deeper Divers among Us: How to Use Quantitative Strategies to Enhance Fundamental Valuations," explores two case studies that do just that. However, this book does not cover techniques to do deep analysis into individual companies.[2]

Horizons (or Rebalancing Frequency)

A key part of any quantitative investing screen is the horizon of the strategy. If the screen provides information that determines what the trade will be, the horizon provides the duration over which the information in the screen is valid. After the horizon is reached, the old positions are closed out, and if desired, the screen can be run again and new positions chosen. This process of closing out old positions and choosing new ones is known as *rebalancing*. The horizon of your strategy is, thus, also known as the *rebalancing period*. Rebalancing is a very important part of quantitative investing and Chapter 8, "Rebalancing—Why, How, and How Often," is dedicated to this concept.

Many times, the measures used in the screen dictate the horizon. So, for example, in the screen discussed earlier that was based on unemployment, the strategy must have a horizon of at least one month because unemployment numbers are released monthly. Put a different way, horizons cannot be shorter than the frequency at which information is released (if they were, the stocks in the screen would remain the same until new information came out). The screens based on PE ratios can have a much shorter horizon because the price of a stock is constantly changing and, thus, PE ratios are constantly changing.

If the trading horizon is longer than the information frequency, you risk that the information previously used to generate the portfolio has gone stale in between rebalances. For example, you sort on PE ratios today and buy all stocks with PE between 0 and 10. Tomorrow, one of the stocks you bought spikes, its PE is more than 10 and no longer passes through your screen. If your horizon is longer than a day, you will hold this stock despite the fact that the stock no longer passes through your screen. Thus, the shorter the horizon, the less likely stocks that are in your portfolio that do not pass through your screen, and the less likely that your portfolio excludes stocks that have evolved to satisfy the criteria of the screen.

The other main factor driving strategy horizon is transaction costs. The shorter the horizon of your strategy, the more times you will have to trade out of old positions and into new ones. Trading generally incurs transactions costs, both in terms of commissions, price impact when trading, and time and headache spent executing your trades.

This is the main tension in choosing the ideal strategy horizon. Too long and you're holding stocks based on old information; too short and your returns are being eroded by transaction costs. In the financial industry, trading horizons can range from the extremely long (a year or even longer) to the very, very short (microseconds or even nanoseconds). High-frequency trading is the form of quantitative "investing" that deals with these very short holding periods. However, high-frequency trading really is not "investing" because positions are rarely held overnight and rarely is the intention of such trades to actually invest in companies. This book, for most strategies, runs a quarterly rebalance. Equities Lab (the tool that most of the analysis in this book uses) has a default rebalancing period of a week, although that can be easily changed.

Backtesting

Once you've decided how you want your strategy to look in terms of screens and horizons, you have to backtest it. To *backtest* a strategy is to see how it would have performed had it been implemented historically.

For example, if your strategy were to buy stocks with PE ratios between 0 and 10, rebalancing every week, you would need to go back to each week historically, see what stocks would pass the screen, and hold them equally in your portfolio. At the end of the week, you would sell all the stocks and reinvest the proceeds into the new stocks that would pass your screen for the next week. Along the way, you would keep track of the cumulative returns to the strategy. The results of your backtest would look like Figure 1.2.

Figure 1.2 Backtest of 0 to 10 PE strategies

These are results from Equities Lab. The darker (lower) line is the return of the S&P 500; the lighter (upper) line is the return of your strategy. We discuss how to use Equities Lab to generate these types of backtests in Chapter 2, "What You Need to Start Investing Using Quantitative Techniques." Before that, I want to point out a few things about the backtest results. In this particular case, I chose a ten-year time period over which to backtest. At the beginning of each week, Equities Lab chooses all stocks with a PE of more than 0 and less than 10 and creates a portfolio, holding an equal amount of each stock. It holds this portfolio until the end of the week and then sells all holdings, reinvesting the proceeds equally into the stocks chosen by the screen for the following week.[3]

In this backtest, you are looking at the returns to a trading strategy following the screen compared with the returns to the S&P 500 index. Over the ten years, $100 invested in this simple quantitative trading strategy would have returned about $275 in profits.[4] The same $100 invested in the S&P 500 would have returned about $110 in profits.

And just like that, you have your first quantitative equity investing strategy. You will invest in stocks that have between 0 and 10 PE ratios, rebalancing your portfolio each week. Doing this historically would have outperformed the market by a healthy amount over the last decade, and if this pattern were to continue over the next ten years, you'd be rich! Richer, anyway.

Implementation

Implementation is the most important part of the whole process, but once you have a strategy, it is generally easy to do. For example, if you chose a strategy such that you are investing in stocks with PE ratios between 0 and 10, all you'd have to do is open a brokerage account and divide your money equally between the stocks returned by the screen.

In theory, it sounds easy, but in practice, myriad complexities would arise, most of which are specific to a given individual. For example, the screen might return 500 stocks, but you only have $5,000 to invest, making it cost-inefficient to divide your capital evenly between the screened names.[5] Some of the more common concerns (such as quantitative investing with limited capital) are addressed in Chapter 14, "How Do You Actually Make Money Now? A Brief Guide to Implementation."

✳✳✳

So we've outlined the general steps for devising a quantitative investment strategy: screen, backtest, and implement. However, numerous specific questions remain. These could include the following:

1. How do I get started developing my own strategies?

2. Why did you choose stocks with PE between 0 and 10?

3. What if I look at other backtesting horizons (for example, five years instead of ten years)?

4. Why is the rebalancing period a week?

---

5. Why am I comparing my strategy against the S&P 500?

6. Can't I find a strategy that does better than this in backtesting?

These, and other, questions are what the rest of this book is about. Chapter 2 discusses the tools needed to help you start creating and backtesting your own quantitative strategies (Question 1) before the rest of the book fills in the answers to the other questions.

Endnotes

1. This is known in industry and academic circles as a *momentum* screen. The screen buys winners in the hope they continue to be winners (or the *momentum* continues). Narasimhan Jegadeesh and Sheridan Titman documented it in their 1993 article, "Returns to Buying Winners and Selling Losers: Implications for Stock Market Efficiency" (Jegadeesh & Titman, 1993).

2. An excellent reference for this is *Security Analysis* (Graham & Dodd, 1934). There are many revised versions of this text and other similar texts available. However, even Graham himself admitted such deep fundamental analysis is unlikely to yield the same payoffs in the modern markets that it did at the time the book was written (Graham, 1976).

3. Equally weighting stocks that pass through the screen is a very common practice and is the only weighting scheme currently supported in Equities Lab backtests. However, there are other ways to weight stocks in the portfolio. Weighting is discussed in Chapter 9, "Weights—Equal or Otherwise."

4. Of course, this is assuming zero transaction costs. In practice, weekly rebalancing would lead to many trades and high transactions costs, which, in turn, would erode returns.

5. Often, tickers or companies are also referred to as *names.* If you use this terminology, not only will you have another synonym for ticker/company, but you'll also sound like you are in tune with the asset management industry.

2

What You Need to Start Investing Using Quantitative Techniques

egardless of who you are and how your interest in quantitative investing is likely to manifest, you will require a few things (in addition to this book) to begin your journey. These are as follows:

- Money (don't worry too much if you don't have this yet)

- Time

- A base level of interest, intelligence, and computer literacy

- A brokerage account

- A computer

- Data and software

What you have in each category will probably impact how exactly you choose to pursue a quantitative investing agenda in a way that only you can determine. For now, this chapter just outlines why and how each of these things is important to a quantitative investing platform.

Money

How much do you need to start investing quantitatively? I'd argue that if you have a few thousand dollars, given the right time horizon (which almost everyone has), that it's worth learning how to do it yourself. Commissions can be as low as a few dollars per trade, and there's a wealth of free information available. The free trial of Equities Lab software that comes with this book will give you the tools to devise a strategy that works for you.

If you don't have any money now, but expect to have some in the future—that describes almost all students—then you should still learn how to invest. You've got the time to learn now, and you might not have as much time when you have more money (probably from working). That's one of the cruel ironies of life.

Time

Quantitative investing requires time in two ways. The first is straightforward: You need to have some time to read this book, develop strategies, determine how to implement those strategies, and so on. This is not a large amount of time, and by the fact that you're already a few pages deep into this book, I'll assume you have some of this. I call this sort of time *labor time*. The second is the time you need for your quantitative strategy to start showing results. I'll call this *investment time*.

Labor Time

How many hours does it take to learn quantitative investing? How many hours per week does it take to actually implement a successful quantitative trading strategy? I could tell you that you could just use existing strategies (such as buying value stocks, as described in the "Value Screener" section in Chapter 3, "Creating a Screen—The Nuts and Bolts of Choosing a Quantitative Investing Strategy"), and if they work as well in the future as they did in the past, you'd be able to be up and running in less than five to ten hours, and maintain the strategy with a minimal outlay of about three to four hours per quarter (or however frequently you choose to rebalance).

However, it's likely that after reading this book you'll want to trade a strategy that is your own. You'll want to understand it, tweak it, and improve it. You'll also want to improve it as you learn from experience. For example, you might not want to repeat that unfortunate experience where you invested in a financial company that matched the screen, only to realize that you didn't understand how banks' financial statements are very different from financial statements of typical companies.

As you read this book and your understanding improves, and as you become familiar with Equities Lab (or whatever data/software you choose to use), you'll want to create new screens and modify existing ones. Doing that (and learning how) takes time. I'm not going to put an upper bound on how long until you are a master quantitative investor. I'm going on three degrees in finance (a bachelor's, a master's, and a doctorate), half a decade in industry, and half a decade in academia, and I'm still learning more about the process every year! That being said, I will hopefully give you a headstart by distilling the most important bits of what I've picked up on my journey to writing this book.

Investment Time

The second way you will need time is the time you need for your quantitative strategy to start showing results. How much time is enough? More is obviously better than less. A lot depends on when you are likely to need the money. Are you going to spend it all a week from now, or is it intended for your grandchildren's retirement accounts?

In general, people underestimate how long their horizon is. If you're married, you have the maximum life expectancy of you and your spouse to work with. Do you have children, or do you plan to have them? There's yet a longer investment horizon. Even if you are 70, and of average health, you'll likely live to 91. That's 21 years, assuming you don't count a bequest to your descendants. No matter how you slice it, your investment horizon is generally close to or longer than a quarter century. For most people, it's longer than half a century. You don't need to plan that far ahead, but you definitely do not need to sit in cash for 50 years.

Granted, if you have a big cash outflow coming up soon, your effective investment horizon might be shorter as a result. For example, if you're planning to buy a house in the next ten years or pay for your children's college, there is some merit to tailoring investments for a shorter investment horizon. Any horizon more than five years is perfectly fine for implementing a quantitative strategy. In fact, even with a year or two, you can start trying out quantitative strategies. If you like them and they work well with your temperament, you'll likely find yourself continuing beyond the initial period. Making large sums of money in a matter of days, weeks, or, months is *not* an appropriate goal for the quantitative strategies this book addresses. There are plenty of "get-rich-quick systems" out there for you. I don't recommend them, but it's your choice.

> *"Compound interest is the eighth wonder of the world. He who understands it, earns it...he who doesn't...pays it."*
> —Albert Einstein

A long time horizon is important mainly because of the power of compounding. The law of compound interest has been described as the eighth wonder of the world, and a few examples will illustrate why. First, let's start with cash. Cash has typically underperformed inflation by about 3% annually. If you have an investment horizon of 33 years, your $1,000 today will buy $360 after inflation's done eroding it. If you invest in bonds, your return would be better—outperforming inflation by 2%. That is in a historic bond bull market that saw interest rates fall from 20% to nothing today.[1] Disregarding the overly optimistic bond returns portrayed by falling interest rates, your $1,000 in bonds would become $1,922 in 33 years. That's good, but not as good as equities. The stock market has historically (over the last 100 years or so) performed about 7% above inflation. That turns your $1,000 into $9,325. That's five times as much as the bond markets.

But we're not done yet. Let's assume you take that as a baseline, and imagine quantitative investing techniques can further help you outperform the market by a measly 3%. Now your $1,000 becomes about $23,000, inflation adjusted. How about an outperformance over the markets of 5%? You'd get $42,000 in 33 years! Because 33 years is too long to imagine, and who knows what the world will look like, let's imagine you outperform by 10% over 10 years. That would be $4,800 versus the $2,000 the market would give you. That is the power of time, given the right quantitative investing strategy.

A Base Level of Interest, Intelligence, and Computer Literacy

The fact that you picked this book up indicates you are interested. Even if you put the book back right now, and stop reading—it's too late. You've already indicated a willingness to deal with numbers, and some curiosity. That's it. That's all you need. If you can use Excel well, you're ahead of the pack, and following the software solutions that are described in this guide should be easy. Equities Lab is the main software solution this book uses. It is more intuitive than standard coding packages that some readers may find intimidating. It is also powerful enough to code almost any strategy you could potentially be interested in. This book, together with the software, should hopefully make the process of developing, backtesting, and implementing your quantitative strategies relatively painless.

A Brokerage Account

You will need a brokerage account to invest in stocks. Which one? I won't dictate—individual tastes vary. This book does, however, include a section on the pros and cons of various brokerages out there (see Chapter 14, "How Do You Actually Make Money Now? A Brief Guide to Implementation"). If you already have a brokerage account that charges reasonable commissions, and you are happy with it, it will be easy enough to use it to start your quantitative investing agenda. You can optimize and find the right account after you've decided whether quantitative investing is a good fit for you. If you don't have a brokerage account yet, it is easy enough to open one with any of the discount online brokerages by filling out a few forms and mailing a check (or cutting an e-check or using an ACH transfer from your bank account if you are familiar with these).

A Computer

You don't need a multiscreen wonder that you see traders using in the movies. Nor do you need an eight-core gaming rig to use Equities Lab.[2] However, you will need more than a tablet, and a newer Windows machine will serve you well. Apple machines should also be fine, but some might give you a bit of trouble during the Equities Lab installation.[3] Excel, of course, will work just fine on any of these platforms.

Data and Software

Data and software are essential to quantitative investing. When you invest, you are buying a stock at a price, expressed as a number. You hope that the number will increase, so you can sell it at a profit. Although humans are relatively good at processing prices for a single good (or stock) quickly and well, processing prices for the entire universe of stocks is a bit too much for our brains. We need help. Specifically, we need software and data to help in the following areas.

Stock Screeners

Finding a small list of stocks to look through is the job of a stock screener. There are thousands of stocks out there, and most of them are simply unsuitable—too big, too small, too speculative, whatever. Screening is a core process in quantitative investing. There are free screeners on the Web that offer little more than taking a collection of known values and insisting that your candidates fall between X and Y for each of the values. (For example, Google Finance has a lovely stock screener, shown in Figure 2.1, that does exactly this and is available at https://www.google.com/finance/stockscreener.) Equities Lab also allows you to screen stocks, but does so with many added pieces of functionality. For example, you can set screens to select top-ranked stocks by any metric, or even to select top-ranked stocks in a given metric in a specific industry. It doesn't matter which screener you choose, so long as it does the job you need it to.

Backtesting

Backtesting is where the pedal really meets the metal in software and data requirements. Basically, it's a combination of the stock screener and historical stock data and prices. The software and data must be able to simulate running the screen you choose historically and show you how it would have performed had you run the screen in the past. Essentially, you are testing the screen on the past (hence, the name *backtest*). This might seems daunting, but the included software should make this much easier than it sounds.

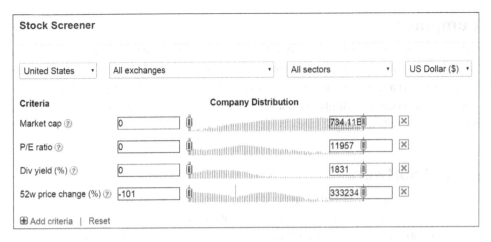

Figure 2.1 Google Finance stock screener (from Google)

Information for the Stock Deep Dive

Most of the time, you'll have a set of names generated by your screener. You might even have two sets of names, one for stocks that you like and another for stocks you really dislike (and may want to short sell). Although quantitative screens are great, you might also want to find out more about a company before making a trade. Many of the items that show up in a deep dive are likely to be qualitative: Did management seem honest in the last conference call? Are they dependent on a single, large customer? It will require good old-fashioned sleuthing to find answers to these questions. The Web is your friend. Some companies have investor relations departments where you can ask questions. These investor relation departments generally don't respond favorably to calls from smaller, retail investors, but you might succeed in contacting them.

I also like reading about a stock in SeekingAlpha, Yahoo!, and Google Finance forums to see what the investment community is like. Excessive exuberance and mindless devotion can give me a warning that a stock will be very volatile, sort of like a fad. Data is obviously important for this deep dive analysis, but software is as well, as you will need to organize your thoughts about all the companies that you are interested in. Any good tool will work, including Excel.

Stock News

Your brokerage account will likely feature some news about any given company you ask about. Google and Yahoo! Finance are helpful here as well. Any of these sites allow you to set up an e-mail alert for news from a set of companies you are monitoring. That way, you'll always be abreast of the most recent developments for companies in your screen.

The good news is this book comes with a piece of software and data that allows you to perform a wide range of analyses to support your quantitative investing agenda. As for the other things you need, you should have most of them readily available. And for those of you who don't have a lot of money yet, don't worry: Just learn the techniques and when the money comes in, you'll be ready to start investing quantitatively.

A Data and Software 2-in-1: Equities Lab

The main problem with developing quantitative investing strategies (until now) has been that it requires a lot of data and the coding ability to parse and analyze the data. Most hedge funds hire PhDs in disciplines ranging from computer science to statistics to physics to finance in order to obtain the requisite skills to launch quantitative investing strategies.

Even the simple strategies outlined in Chapter 1, "Overview of Quantitative Investing"—for example, investing in stocks with PE ratios between 0 and 10—would require a fair amount of data merging and coding. First, you would have to obtain daily stock prices for the last ten years. Then, using accounting statements for the last ten years, you would have to obtain the number of shares outstanding quarterly, as well as the quarterly earnings. Then, once you have computed the PE ratios for these companies over time (PE ratio equals total market capitalization, or price per share multiplied by the number of shares, divided by earnings over the last year), you would have to compute average returns of the screened stocks each week. It would take an experienced coder hours of mind-numbing work to merge and clean the data, and a bit longer to generate code to backtest the strategy. Most investors simply do not have the time or inclination to do this.

The good news is this book comes with a 20-week trial subscription to Equities Lab, which does all the data merging and provides an intuitive natural language–based programming interface to generate and backtest screens.[4] The bad news is that once you're hooked after the trial, you'll need to buy a license to Equities Lab or start doing the hard work of merging data and coding screens yourself.

Getting an Equities Lab Account and Logging In

If you bought a new copy of this book, you will receive a 20-week free subscription to Equities Lab. The easiest way to set up your account is simply to forward the electronic copy of your receipt (your receipt or order confirmation from Amazon, for example) to education@equitieslab.com. An account with your username (which will be the email address the receipt is sent from) and a generated password will be sent to you within 24 hours. You can use this information to sign in to your account at www.equitieslab.com using the Your Account tab.

Once you have signed in with your account, you can change your stock password if you want. You will also find instructions to download and install Equities Lab. See Figure 2.2 for how your screen should look after logging in and while you're downloading the software in Windows. Simply click and run the downloaded executable when you are ready.

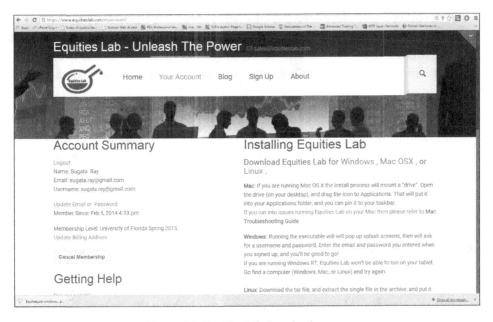

Figure 2.2 Equities Lab download screen

If you do not have an electronic receipt, you can still obtain a login using the code at the back of this book. Go to http://www.equitieslab.com/book, which will redirect you to an Equities Lab sign-up page that looks like Figure 2.3. Enter your information, email address (which will also be your username), and your password. You have to enter the coupon code on the front flap of the dust jacket of this book in the Coupon Code field in order to get the 20-week trial. Note that if you use this second method to create an account, you have to enter your credit card information, and you will be charged a nominal $1 processing fee for your free trial. If you do not have a coupon code, you will be charged the regular rate for the 20-week membership. Note that if you use this method to get your subscription, your subscription is automatically renewed at the end of the 20 weeks unless you cancel the subscription. (You can do this from the base Your Account page shown in Figure 2.2.)

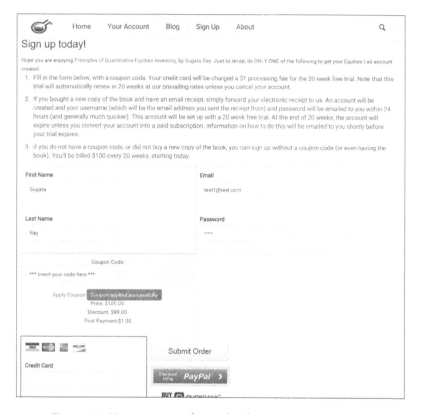

Figure 2.3 How to get your free trial without an electronic receipt

Creating Your First Screen

Now that you've downloaded and installed Equities Lab, you are ready to create your first screen. If you are looking at the main home page, you should see the image shown in Figure 2.4. Note that as Equities Lab is constantly being updated, some minor details might be different in the version of Equities Lab that loads up compared with the screenshots. However, the screenshots and videos should help you follow the basics.

Before you go on reading, you may want to watch the video (see Video 2.1) embedded in the bottom panel of the home page. It will probably do more to familiarize you with Equities Lab than reading pages of text and screenshots. There are a lot of features in

Equities Lab; don't feel overwhelmed by the intro video. Videos in the following sections are much more precise and deal with a single feature at a time.

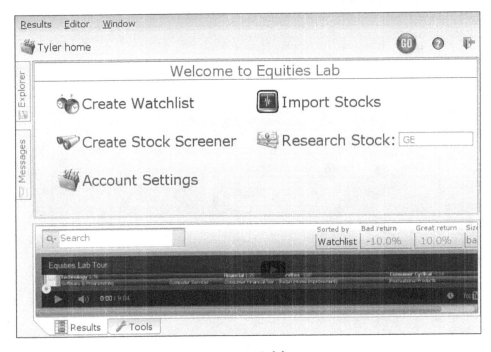

Figure 2.4 Equities Lab home page

TIP

The videos in this book (and others) are available at videos.sugata.in. The link will redirect to a YouTube video channel that has videos associated with the book, as well as other videos on quantitative investing strategies using Equities Lab.

VIDEO 2.1

 Equities Lab intro video: http://bookvid21.sugata.in

To create your first screener, click on Create Stock Screener in the middle of the left column to start the stock screener interface. You should see a screen that looks like Figure 2.5.

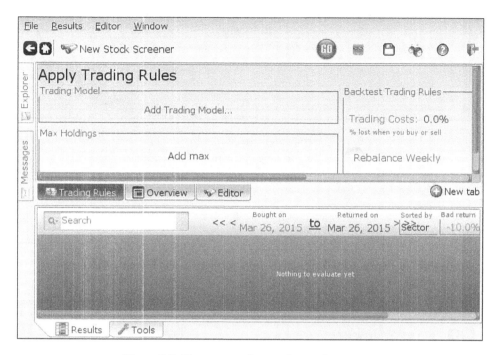

Figure 2.5 Home screen for creating stock screeners

Don't worry too much about the information here; jump straight to the Editor tab. This is the main tab where you will be coding screens. Let's use the example mentioned previously, where we want to create a screen that invests in companies with a PE ratio greater than 0 and less than 10. Simply type in $0 < PE < 10$ into the box. Press Enter and Equities Lab should accurately parse it into the criteria you are interested in, as shown in Figure 2.6.

Video on creating your first screen: http://bookvid22.sugata.in

To see the names of the stocks of the companies that fit this requirement, click on the GO button in the upper right and then click on the Results tab located in the lower-left corner of your screen (see Figure 2.7).

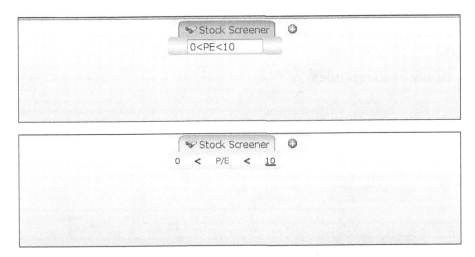

Figure 2.6 Typing something into the stock screener and how Equities Lab parses it

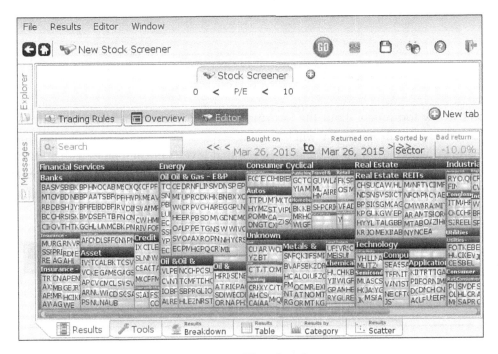

Figure 2.7 Filtered results

Many ticker symbols pass the 0 to 10 PE screens. If you were to change any property in your stock screener, the number of companies that appear could differ. Notice the middle part of the screen, which states the filter date and results date. This refers to the date on which the results were filtered and the period over which returns were computed for these filtered stocks. In this case, both dates are the same (today). That is why all the tickers are gray—the returns over this period (essentially 0 days) are all 0.

When you create a new screen, the filter date automatically chooses your current date, meaning it screens for stocks that pass through the screen today. To change the dates in which you filter your stock screener, simply click on the dates to change them. In Figure 2.8, I screened for stocks that passed through the screen about a year ago.

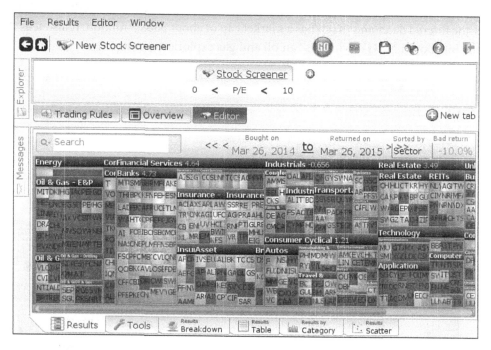

Figure 2.8 Heat map for results filtered a year ago with performance to today

The colors and names listed in the *heat map* suddenly changed from gray names to a variety of red, green, or gray boxes. Equities Lab will also inform you of how these stocks, overall, performed in the last year in a Results Overview box that vanishes after a few seconds (and is hence not in the screenshot) and you are free to assess your screen results.

Results Explained

Hover your mouse over any company in the heat map for a display box to appear and inform you of the market cap and score of the security. The score is the percent change in closing price from the *filtered on* date to the *scored on* date. In creating Figure 2.9, I hovered over LNCGY. The box that appears informs me that the LNCGY lost 55.49% over the filtered dates and that it has a market cap of about $508.5 million. It also tells me a little bit about LNCGY, which is "an oil and gas exploration company."

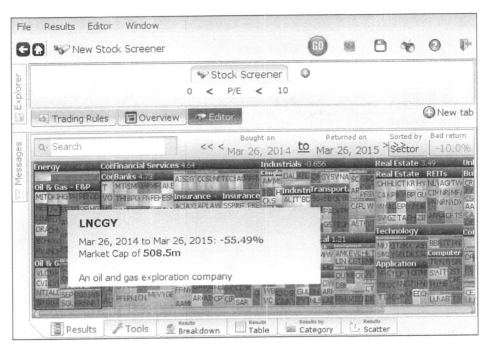

Figure 2.9 Getting information for each ticker in the screen

If you then click the ticker, more information will appear and you can do further research on any company that passes your screen in this manner. If at any time you want to zoom in to better read the box names, simply double-click on any company in the heat map. I double-clicked on BP, and my new display looked like Figure 2.10.

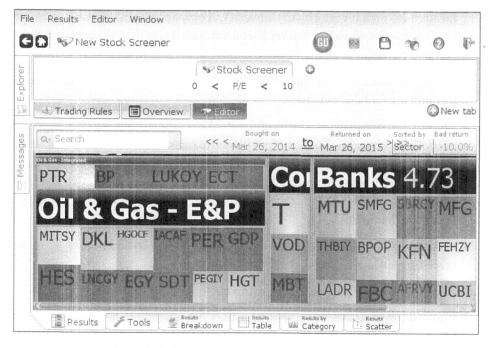

Figure 2.10 Zooming in to a particular sector or industry

I could keep zooming in or I could choose to right-click on the sector labels (the blue bars above the heat map that have the sector names on them) and click on Drill Up, which will zoom my display back out to what it looked like before I zoomed in. There's also a shortcut where you can simply click the up arrow to Drill Up (zoom out of the heat map), or click the down arrow to Drill Down into whatever sector you are hovering over (zoom further into the heat map).

Feel free to click on the various tabs located at the bottom of the screen as well. The Results Breakdown tab displays pie charts to analyze the results found in your stock screener. This provides breakdowns of the screened tickers in terms of a variety of characteristics, including the following:

- **Market capitalization**—The fraction of companies that are small cap, large cap, and so on.

- **Beta**—A measure of sensitivity to market conditions. Most stocks are somewhat sensitive to the market. However, the level of sensitivity varies. Companies with a higher beta do better than the market when the market goes up and worse than the market when it goes down. Conversely, companies with lower betas do better than the market when the market goes down and worse than the market when the market goes up.

- **EPS**—Also known as earnings per share, the measure of dollars of earnings (net income) attributable per share.

- **PE**—The price to earnings ratio of the stocks in your screen. As you can see, our portfolio has only low and very low PE companies. This is by design, as we filter out all companies with a PE above 10. As a reference, the average PE of the market typically varies between 15 and 20. Companies that are cheap relative to earnings have PEs less than that, and companies that are expensive relative to earnings have PEs more than that.

- **Volume**—The measure of shares traded, both as of today and over the preceding 30 days.

- **Yield**—The dividend yield of the company.

- **Piotroski F-score**—A score that measures the quality, or health, of companies' financial metrics. See Chapter10"Some Powerful Screens," for details on this.

- **Sector**—The industry breakdown of stocks in your screener.

To change the breakdowns presented, you can click on the Synopsis tab (as shown in Figure 2.11) and choose something else, but for now, let's move on to other data we can get from Equities Lab.

The Results Table tab has the companies that are in the screen in tabular form and ready to be exported into Excel, as shown in Figure 2.12. This is the primary mechanism by which to export results of your screen to do further analysis in Excel or to use the output to guide your trading decisions.

Clicking on the bottom Category tab to the right of Table displays the results in bar graph form. The default view is holdings by sector (shown in Figure 2.13), but you can change that view by clicking on the Sector link on the right side of the screen. This is essentially a bar chart form of the results displayed in the pie chart in Figure 2.11. Similarly, you can also have breakdowns by market capitalization (see Figure 2.14).

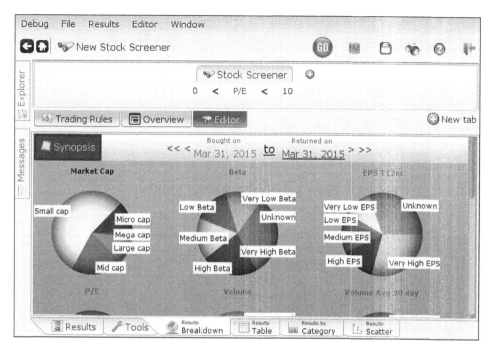

Figure 2.11 Breakdown of stocks returned by the screener

Ticker	Company	Return	Close	Market ...	Change...	Sector	Indu
TENG	Trans Energy	-52	3.8	50.67m	-2.56%	Energy	Oil &
GECR	Georgia Car...	71.93	14.25	51.23m	-0.35%	Financial Se...	Banks
OEPC	Q EP	-12.2	18.52	51.27m	-2.47%	Unknown	Buildi
VYFC	Valley Finan...	77.68	11.2	52.66m	0.81%	Financial Se...	Banks
KFS	Kingsway Fi...	39.7	4.07	53.52m	3.24%	Financial Se...	Insur
NASGF	Northstar A...	0	1.81	54.2m	0%	Industrials	Aeros
GNK...	Genco Ship...	-40.08	1.3	54.25m	2.7%	Industrials	Trans
SGOC	SGOCO Gro...	-83.39	3.22	54.93m	-6.43%	Technology	Comp
MBCN	Middlefield ...	18.08	28	54.97m	3.32%	Financial Se...	Banks
SWBC	Sunwest Ba...	15.15	33,000	55.9m	0%	Financial Se...	Banks
EDS	Exceed Co	-10.35	1.73	56.31m	0%	Consumer ...	Manu
CWBC	Community ...	-6.53	6.98	57.03m	-2.25%	Financial Se...	Banks
VSCI	Vision-Scie...	-60.5	1.25	57.7m	-19.37%	Healthcare	Medic
CSUN	China Sune...	-59.59	4.38	58.57m	-19.76%	Technology	Semic

Q-

Bought on Mar 26, 2014 **to** Returned on Mar 26, 2015 << < > >> Export

Figure 2.12 The Results Table tab

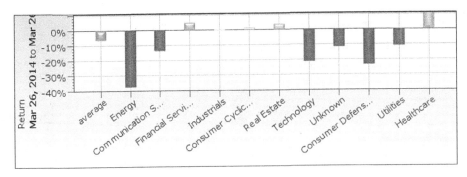

Figure 2.13 Screener results by sector

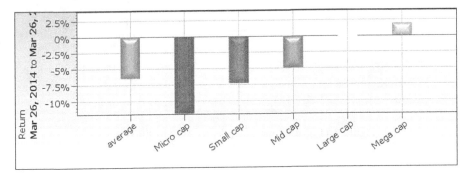

Figure 2.14 Screener results by market capitalization

You can explore the results further. The interface is fairly intuitive. I'll stop belaboring the various analyses you can do on the results and move on to backtesting.

Backtesting

Backtesting allows you to look at the performance of the stock screener as if you had invested using the strategy in the past. You can run the backtest from any of the previous screens. Once you have a screener implemented, move your cursor to the upper right of the screen and click on the square icon located to the right of the GO icon (circled in Figure 2.15).

Once you begin to run the backtest, a box like the one shown in Figure 2.16 appears. This simply confirms the backtest range (default is January 1, 2010, to today) and the other parameters of the backtest. Click Run, and the backtest begins.

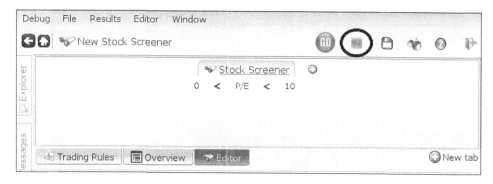

Figure 2.15 How to run a backtest—click the square icon that looks like a chart to the right of the GO button

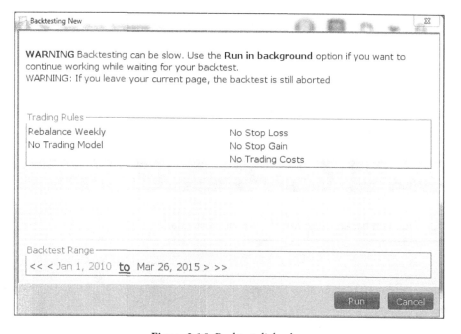

Figure 2.16 Backtest dialog box

Backtests can take a while to run, depending on the complexity of your screen, so if you want to continue working while the backtest runs, a Run in Background option is available. When the results are ready, you can examine a backtest graph, similar to the one shown in Figure 2.17.

Figure 2.17 Backtest results

This screen has largely followed the market since January 2010. In addition to a graph of cumulative returns during the backtest period, other analyses are presented in the back-test tabs below the graph. Click on them to explore. Video 2.4 goes through the different types of analysis you can do in backtests.

At this point, I'm sure a number of readers will put this guide down and start tinkering around with Equities Lab. Go ahead. I'll be right here when you return.

VIDEO 2.4

 Video on backtesting: http://bookvid24.sugata.in

TIP

Equities Lab and the data underlying it are dynamic. It is constantly being improved, and the data underlying it are changing, both as new financial data is added, but also as data errors are corrected. It is quite likely that results you obtain will be slightly different, even if you rerun the exact screen for the exact same data. This is a fairly common issue in empirical analysis of quantitative strategies. Just double-check overall trends that are similar and do not be overly alarmed by small differences.

Endnotes

1. Bond prices rise as rates fall. Imagine buying a bond for a hundred dollars that pays a 5% interest rate per year, forever. These are called perpetual bonds, or consols. This pays $5 a year. Now imagine that rates fall to 2.5%. Because these things pay $5 a year, the value of a bond has to rise to $200, to make the $5 interest payment equal to the new interest rate of 2.5% ($5/$200 = 2.5% interest per year).

2. Equities Lab is run on a cloud server, so having a faster PC actually will not significantly improve Equities Lab's performance.

3. Apple generally likes to tightly control the user environment on their Macs. This is good for a lot of things, but sometimes leads to problems with Java-based programs. Equities Lab is a Java-based program. That being said, you should be able to install Equities Lab on a Mac, and it should work fine. If you have trouble installing Equities Lab onto your Mac (or PC), e-mail support@equitieslab.com and you should be able to get the help you need. There is also a troubleshooting guide for the Equities Lab installation process on www.equitieslab.com.

4. This book includes a 20-week trial. After the trial ends, options for a discounted longer-term subscription plan will also be available.

3

Creating a Screen—The Nuts and Bolts of Choosing a Quantitative Investing Strategy

O nce you've gotten accustomed to Equities Lab and explored its functionality, the next question you must ask yourself is: What exactly am I trying to accomplish? Purpose is paramount in quantitative investing and simply screening for a group of criteria without any clearly-articulated purpose will probably not produce a good outcome.

Investing Goals and Linking Them to Screens

The easiest way to think about investing goals is to think about what you're trying to do when you are investing. Make money? Sure. Everyone who's investing is trying to make money. But is there something more specific you are trying to accomplish? For example, perhaps you're devising a strategy for your elderly relatives, who have saved a tidy amount and are trying to convert their savings into a steady stream of cash flow. Or perhaps you are trying to make money, but you want to make sure that you aren't too badly hurt during a market downturn.

It will probably take a full finance degree to learn the skill of converting goals into observable metrics. However, Table 3.1 lists a few common goals and associated screeners so you have something to begin with.

Table 3.1 Investing Goals and Associated Screeners

Goal	Screeners
Income generating—good for investors looking to receive a steady stream of cash flow from their capital	Screen for high dividend-paying stocks. Specifically, look for companies that have a high dividend yield (Dividend_Yield in Equities Lab). *Dividend yield* is defined as the sum of dividends paid over the last year divided by the price of the stock. Just for context, the average dividend yield of companies in the S&P 500 is about 2%. A good high yield strategy should be paying out about 5%.
Making money, but not suffering too badly in a downturn	Screen for stocks with low beta, perhaps industries you think will weather bad markets better, or perhaps large cap stocks that are more stable during rough times. *Beta* is a theoretical measure of how sensitive a company is to market conditions. A beta of 1 means the stock should move up and down in lockstep with the markets. Positive betas less than 1 mean the stock still moves with the market but will not move as much as the market. Positive betas more than 1 move with the markets, but more. Negative beta stocks (these are very rare) move inversely with the markets. As an example, these would be predicted returns of stocks with various betas if the market moves up or down by 1%.

	$\beta = -\frac{1}{2}$	$\beta = \frac{1}{2}$	$\beta = 1$	$\beta = 1\frac{1}{2}$
Market up 1%	−0.5%	0.5%	1%	1.5%
Market down 1%	0.5%	−0.5%	−1%	−1.5%

Goal	Screeners
Making money by buying under-valued stocks, which will rise as the market realizes the true value of their earnings stream	This is the classic value screen and one that we will discuss extensively throughout the book. This is the screen of choice for legendary value investors such as Warren Buffett and Joel Greenblatt. In fact, Joel Greenblatt's Magic Formula, which is described in his book, *The Little Book That Beats the Market* (Greenblatt, 2005), is a screen that exemplifies the value screen: It looks for companies trading cheap relative to earnings and companies with high return on capital. In broad terms, successful value screens will look for companies with a lot of earnings (or other sources of cash flow, including liquidation value), which are trading cheaply relative to the cash flow. PE ratios and price-to-book ratios are often used to screen for such stocks.

Goal	Screeners
Going for home runs—making money by picking stocks with the highest probability of generating very high returns	This is the opposite of a value screen. Whereas value stocks are those for which each current dollar of earnings or book value can be bought for cheap, these stocks are likely to trade at high PE and price to book (or PB) ratios. This is because these stocks are growing fast, and although current earnings may be low relative to the valuation, the hope is that they will grow significantly, justifying the current valuation, and hopefully even pushing it higher. Historically, growth stocks have underperformed value stocks. However, there may still be good reasons to invest in growth stocks. For example, if you are in a high tax bracket and do not plan on selling equities for a long time, growth stocks are great because they typically do not pay dividends (they reinvest any earned money to accelerate their growth).
Going for equity stubs that may have value	Equity stubs are a common investment strategy for deep dive, fundamental value investors. Equity stubs can arise when a company has a lot of cash on hand, where the entire market value of all the shares outstanding is less than the cash on hand. Fundamental investors would say that you're getting the equity stub (the remainder after accounting for the cash on the books) for free when you buy the shares. It is easy to use quantitative tools to screen for companies where the cash on hand is greater than the market value. Of course, investors will then have to figure out why the stock is trading so low, and then decide whether there is likely to be a catalyst that will help remove the reason for the low valuation.
Momentum investing—keep buying current winners and avoiding current losers	Momentum investing is the simple idea that we should invest in winners, while avoiding losers. The opposite investing strategy is contrarian investing (where we invest in losers and avoid current winners). Although these are not investment goals, per se, for the average investor, they may be investment goals for advisors who are managing client money. Advisors like holding winners because these positions are easy to justify: It is easy to justify holding Apple after it has done well for a long period of time. Even if Apple does poorly next year, the position is justifiable to a client. Contrarian positions (buying losers) are often less justifiable if they don't perform, but if they pay off, they make advisors look like geniuses. Screening for these is as simple as looking for the top-performing (or worst-performing) stocks over the last month or year.[1]

Once you have a goal, you can start trying to code a set of rules that help achieve the goal in Equities Lab. The upcoming sections go through three examples, creating a value screener, a dividend yield screener, and a momentum screener. But before that, the following section highlights the dangers of quantitative strategies that do not have a purpose, as well as strategies that are designed solely to outperform on backtests, with no other economic underpinnings.

Aimless Screens

Aimless screens are screens that don't have a clear investing goal in mind. Often, these screens are created with the justification that they have superior backtest results. They often have little economic underpinning, and trading based on them is dangerous.

The best way to show what an aimless screener looks like is to use an example. Figure 3.1 is an example of such a screen—it picks companies with more than 15,000 employees, a depreciation/market cap of more than 20%, and interest expense to long-term debt of more than 3%.

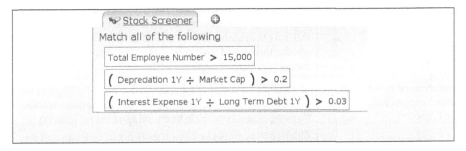

Figure 3.1 Example of a purposeless screen

Although two of these are fine things to be screening for individually (Employees > 15,000 looks for larger companies; interest expense to long-term debt of more than 3% looks for companies that pay a high rate of interest), together they make little sense. Even worse, depreciation/market cap is an odd ratio that makes little sense by itself, let alone when used with other criteria! Depreciation is generally a "book" concept and should be normalized by book values, rather than by market values. There is no coherent reason to use these three criteria together. Additionally, there is no investing goal that all three criteria would help to accomplish.

To see what potential data fields ("properties") are out there, you can either type in some key terms, or hit Ctrl+Shift+P to get a list to choose from.

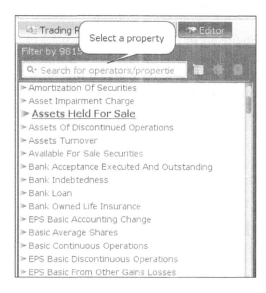

To use an operator on a property (for example, to get Depreciation ÷ Market Cap), click on the first property, and overwrite it with the operator. This puts the operator after the property and creates a blank field if necessary for other properties.

I assigned an extra credit assignment for a class to develop a tradable strategy that beat the market by more than three times in the last ten years and also beat the market in nine of the last ten years. I received many strategies that did well in backtests, but lacked purpose. Watch one of them in Video 3.1.

Of course, in some sense, because I did not ask for screens to be based on any economic fundamentals, my student did exactly the right thing to find a screen that met backtest result objectives, regardless of purpose. Next time, I'll phrase my extra credit assignment better.

Extra credit screener: http://bookvid31.sugata.in

Even if the strategy in Figure 3.1 or the strategy in Video 3.1 produce good results, they lack insight into what made the results good. In fact, if you do run such an aimless screen while experimenting with Equities Lab and find strong performance, I would encourage you to determine what the key driver of the results is. Once you have found the key driver, exclude the other conditions and see if the results are roughly similar. Then, you at least know what drove the outperformance. If the outperformance is fleeting, and disappears with slight changes to the screen, that would suggest that that superior backtest results are simply an artifact of the data, and there is no real reason to expect the outperformance to continue for the screen.

The Problem with Building Strategies Solely to Outperform in Backtests

One might be tempted to believe that good screeners should be designed to maximize backtest performance. (This belief often accompanies the practice of creating screens without a clear investing purpose, but not always.) This is dangerous and should be avoided. I will use an (absurd) example to explain why. Suppose you really like Apple (largely due to stunning returns over the recent past) and decide that companies similar to Apple are going to outperform the market. Here's an example of a screen like this: "I'm going to invest in all companies in the tech sector that have a market cap within 10% of Apple's market cap. If you run this screen and backtest it, you get something similar to what is shown in Figure 3.2.

Looks like a great screen, right? It shows 7x returns, meaning your investment has increased seven-fold (so $1 in this screen would have become $8 by the end). Of course, if you think about the screen a bit more, you realize a big chunk of what is driving these returns is the fact that Apple itself is included in this screen! If you rerun the screen excluding Apple (see Figure 3.3), a very different picture emerges.

This screen does not outperform the market over the ten years. In fact, in the last few years, it has no companies as there are no tech companies with market caps within 10% of Apple's market cap.

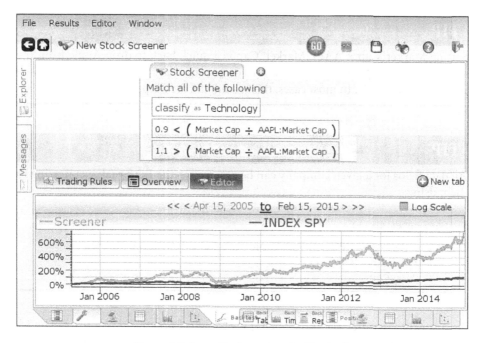

Figure 3.2 Investing in companies like Apple

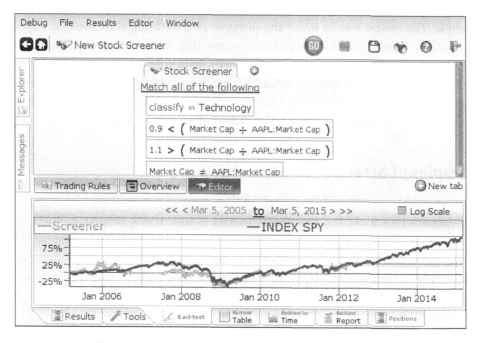

Figure 3.3 Investing in companies like Apple...but *not* Apple

This is a specific manifestation of a general problem known as *overfitting*. The idea is that we are tailoring our investment rules too tightly to what has actually happened. In this case, we chose a trading rule that basically guarantees one home run in the portfolio. Once we remove that known home run, the screen is exposed for the poor strategy it truly is. The easiest way to avoid the problem of overfitting is to have very specific, economically driven goals in mind when constructing screens. Only once you are sure that stocks returned by the screener are actually achieving your goals should you run a backtest to see how the strategy would have performed historically. In fact, it would be perfectly reasonable to invest in a strategy with poor backtest returns, as long as the strategy's backtests show it achieving the goals it set out to achieve.

Examples of Screener Construction

In this section, I construct three basic screeners:

- **Value** —This looks for companies that have low prices, relative to their income or the book value of their assets. The idea is that you're paying a reasonable price for what you are getting. In addition to being written about in many practitioner-oriented publications, this idea was popularized in the academic paper, "The Cross-Section of Expected Stock Returns" (Fama & French, 1992).

- **Momentum**—This is a very simple strategy that winners continue to win. Losers continue to lose. So buy winners and sell losers. The success of this strategy has been documented in the paper, "Returns to Buying Winners and Selling Losers: Implications for Stock Market Efficiency" (Jegadeesh & Titman, 1993). This class of strategies is controversial, and recently there is a sense that it's stopped working well as transaction costs erode a large portion of purported returns.

- **Dividend yield**—This looks for companies that pay a high dividend yield. It is great for investors who are using their equity investments to supplement their income. Dividend yields are often higher than CD rates, so it can provide a nice boost to investment returns. Of course, as opposed to CDs, there is significant risk of capital loss.

Value Screener

Value strategies are among the most common quantitative strategies. In fact, there has been an entire book written simply on quantitative value investing (Gray & Carlisle, 2012). Value stocks are stocks that generate profits or have significant assets that are trading cheaply relative to the profits they generate or the assets they own. It's kind of like buying a twenty dollar bill for less than twenty dollars. This section reviews some basic value-specific criteria, explaining the rationale for the inclusion of each, then continues on to constructing the screener based on these criteria, and concludes with an overview of the results and possible uses for performance data.

Among the most common properties used in such criteria are ratios of price to earnings and book value (also known by the acronyms PE and PB, respectively).

Price to earnings, or PE, ratios are useful because they tell you what you are paying for a unit of earnings. Similar ratios could be price to dividends, or price to revenues (for companies with negative earnings). Similar ratios in other contexts would be the inverse of a CD interest rate (so if you have a rate of 2%, the price of the CD to the cash flow is 50) or the inverse of the rental yield of a piece of real estate.

Price to book, or PB, ratios are useful because they give you a good sense of what assets you're getting for your purchase price. If a company has a big machine that is on the books for $100 million and few liabilities, and the company is trading at $20 million, you'd be getting a great deal on the machine the company held! Of course, buying a few shares doesn't allow you to go and chip a few corners off the machine, but the hope is that once investors realize the company is undervalued relative to the expensive machine it holds, the price of the stock will go up.

The general idea behind value strategies is that *value* stocks (those with low PE and low PB ratios) tend to outperform *growth* stocks (those with high PE and PB ratios). This has been documented in numerous academic studies, although reasons for this outperformance are still the subject of heated debate.

To apply this to your quantitative strategy within Equities Lab, you need to know average PE and PB ratios so you can screen for stocks that have lower than average PE and PB ratios. The PE for the overall market generally hovers between 15 and 20 and the PB hovers between 1.5 and 3.

With that in mind, you can construct a basic value-oriented screener. Typical criteria might include, as mentioned previously, low price to earnings ratios (for example, less than 10) and low price to book ratios (for example, less than 1). First, let's look at the 0 to 10 PE screen, and compare it with similar screens that pick stocks with PEs between 10 to 20, 20 to 30, and 30 to 40.

TIP

To compare backtest results across strategies, create a new tab, titled "plot_any-nameyouwant%." In the tab, insert the backtest operator, and then either type in a strategy (if it's a simple strategy) or refer to a strategy you have created and saved. The % sign makes the scaling for the two charts similar.

```
plot pe10to20%
backtest of 10 < P/E < 20
```

The chart in Figure 3.4 shows that the lower PE ratio stocks have been better investments than the higher PE stocks. I have converted to a log scale (circled in the figure) to ensure return lines are clearly visible. The lower PE slices have outperformed the higher PE slices, and the relationship holds for all slices of PE analyzed. You can also combine PE and PB screens. If you were to screen for both 0 to 10 PEs and 0 to 1 PBs, you would obtain the stocks shown in Figure 3.5.

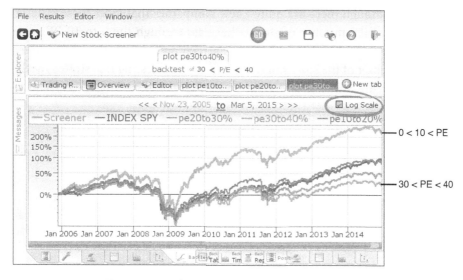

Figure 3.4 Backtest comparison of various PE groups

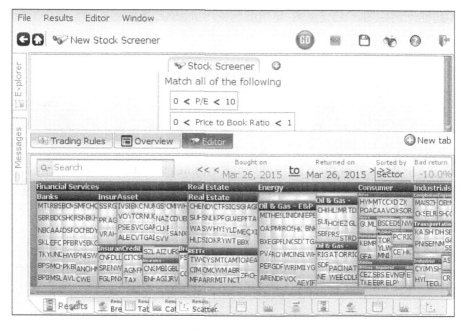

Figure 3.5 Results of basic PE and PB value screen

As you can see, although there are quite a few companies that meet these criteria, this is fewer than either the number of stocks that pass through the 0 to 10 PE screen or the 0 to 1 PB screen. This is because you are screening for both things together, so it ends up being a subset of the stocks in either screen. Backtesting this strategy yields the chart shown in Figure 3.6.

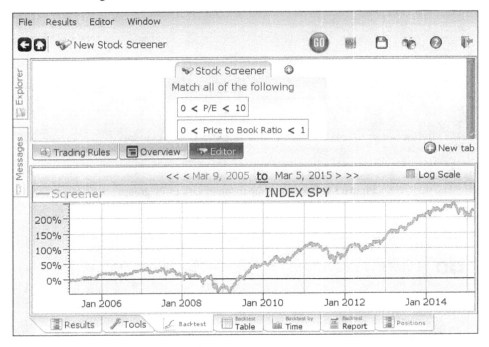

Figure 3.6 Value backtest ten years

As you saw in the case of the 0 to 10 PE strategy, this particular value strategy has also outperformed over the ten-year backtest period. However, the backtest results are very similar to the 0 to 10 PE backtest only. Adding the 0 to 1 PB criteria did not seem to help much.

As it turns out, the PE slices you used turned out to be better discriminators of future performance than the PB slices. From Figure 3.7, you can see that only the 0 to 1 PB slice breaks away from the pack, and that too, only to a limited extent.

The conclusion from this particular analysis is that using the PE screener is sufficient to develop an outperforming value measure. Of course, other PB slices may lead to better results; feel free to try them out.

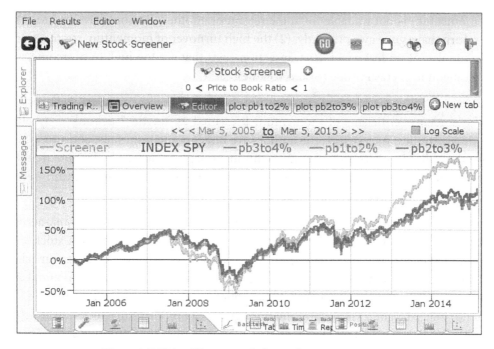

Figure 3.7 Using PB as a stand-alone value screening criteria

Momentum Screener

Momentum screeners are one of a class of technical screeners. Technical screeners are often referred to in the popular media (just think back to quotes in the media where someone mentions a "support level" or a "classic head and shoulders pattern"). Basically, the idea behind technical analysis is that past prices can predict future prices and looking at a price chart can be informative regarding future returns.

In the case of a momentum screener, the analysis is quite easy: If the price has gone up a lot in the past year (the stock has *momentum*), buy; if not, don't buy. Of course, it's a little more complicated than that. For example, what about a good market year (like 2010), when everything went up a lot? One easy way to deal with up-and-down markets is to pick the stocks that performed the best, relative to all other stocks. This is called *relative momentum*.

Momentum has been documented in a number of asset classes in the academic literature, and the concept was popularized by the paper "Returns to Buying Winners and Selling Losers: Implications for Stock Market Efficiency" (Jegadeesh & Titman, 1993). It is also a fairly controversial strategy, as every one to two years, a study pops up saying the momentum is not tradable for some reason or another. Reasons have included (1) the returns have gone away recently, (2) the high turnover of momentum strategies (the large number of trades) generates transaction costs that are too high to overcome, and (3) momentum is crash prone (or too volatile).

The paper "Fact, Fiction and Momentum Investing" has a wonderful discussion of the academic criticisms of momentum presented as "myths," debunked by other aca-demic studies. As a caveat, the authors are huge momentum fans, and run a fund that, from what I understand, uses momentum strategies extensively. Despite that, the piece is informative about the arguments on both sides of the momentum debate (Asness, Frazzini, Israel, & Moskowitz, 2014).

We can generate a relative momentum screen in Equities Lab using the "rank-across" command. The rank-across command returns the percentile rank of each stock with respect to whatever is in the Of field. In this case, it is returns over the last year (close divided by close as of 252 days ago is 1 + last year returns because a year has about 252 trading days).[2] As you can see in Figure 3.8, winners tend to keep outperforming and losers tend to keep lagging. The second and third quartile of momentum stocks are bunched together. Note, however, that (1) this is over 20 years, rather than 10, and (2) this is only for $5 billion market cap stocks, or larger. If you look at results for only the last 10 years (not shown), the momentum quartiles are much closer together and higher momentum stocks actually lag slightly. This is because momentum is prone to high levels of under-performance during crashes, and we experienced a major crash during the last 10 years.[3]

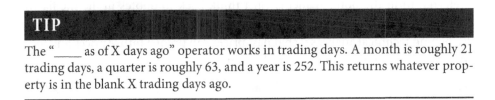

TIP

The "____ as of X days ago" operator works in trading days. A month is roughly 21 trading days, a quarter is roughly 63, and a year is 252. This returns whatever property is in the blank X trading days ago.

Despite the controversy surrounding it, the momentum screen remains popular among academics and practitioners alike. In more recent years, academics have combined momentum and value and have found stocks in the intersection outperform significantly more than either screen alone. See the 2013 paper by Asness, Moskowitz, and Pedersen, "Value and Momentum Everywhere." This intersection is explored in greater detail in Chapter 10, "Some Powerful Screens."

Figure 3.8 Momentum backtests

Dividend Yield Screener

Another common type of screener is a dividend yield screener. This is used by investors who are seeking companies that pay large dividends. Such stocks are favored by retirees and other investors who have capital but who do not have a steady source of income. In addition to generating income from fixed income securities, such investors use dividend-paying stocks to augment their regular income, while also participating in the capital appreciation provided by the equity markets.

The simplest way to screen for high dividend-paying stocks is to use the dividend yield paid in the last year. In Figure 3.9, I picked stocks that paid a dividend yield of between 3% and 5%.[4]

Figure 3.9 Dividend yield screener and plotting divyield

TIP

Any time you want to plot a variable for your screen, create a tab titled "plot_<lowercase descriptive variable name>". In that tab, enter whatever expression you want to be plotted. The average of this variable will be plotted for all stocks in your portfolio in the backtest charts. Additionally, this variable will be in the Backtest Results table that can be exported to Excel.

> plot divyield
> Dividend Yield

The returns to this screen are decent, but nothing to write home about compared with the value screen. In fact, screening for divided yield is somewhat similar to screening for value. However, the main thing I want to point out here is the faint dotted line, graphed against the right axis "divyield." To do this, I created the additional tab "plot_divyield" (circled) using the New Tab button. The average dividend yield on the strategy is about 4% per year. Investors such as retirees, who are interested in a steady stream of cash flow, might be attracted to such stocks.

In backtests in Equities Lab, dividends are instantly and frictionlessly reinvested into the same stock. This is not a bad assumption, but there are other ways to deal with dividends. For example, if the investor was consuming the dividends (spending them on living expenses), you could just look at capital appreciation, ignoring dividends, to see what remains of the capital.

In Equities Lab, the way to toggle between backtesting with dividend reinvesting and dividend consumption is to include a tab titled "dividend_payments" and set the value in the tab as "0." This simply makes backtests report capital gains returns, rather than overall returns, including the dividends, as shown in Figure 3.10.

Figure 3.10 Dividend screener, consuming dividends

Note that the returns are lower (because you are consuming the dividends). The good news is you're still seeing decent returns, while consuming your 4% a year in dividends.

One of the potentially frustrating things about both this screener and the value and momentum screeners are the large number of stocks that the screens return. All the screeners returned more than 300 stocks. This is potentially frustrating because it takes work to buy all these stocks in equal measure. It's even worse if you don't have a lot of money to invest and when dividing the money you have to invest among 300 names is

---

not practical. That is why in most real-life screens, you will want to cap the number of holdings.

Another potentially frustrating thing is that, so far, the backtests have been running with a weekly rebalance. This means that if you wanted to see results similar to those represented in the backtests, you would have to rebalance your portfolio weekly! Realistically, no one will rebalance a portfolio weekly. Quarterly or annual rebalances will give you a more accurate representation of results.

There are other things you need to do as well. For example, among these 300+ stocks, there are bound to be a few extremely illiquid stocks that do not trade more than a few thousand shares a day. Buying these will be difficult, and you should typically devise your screen to exclude these right off the bat.

As a result, you need to put in place a set of exclusions before you start generating stocks with your screener. The following section describes a real-life screener that has exclusions in place to filter out illiquid stocks and the like, and then extends that screener to limit holdings to a manageable number.

A Real-Life Screener

As discussed previously, the value, momentum, and dividend screeners are appealing, but are pretty simplistic. Figure 3.11 shows a real-life screener that I have used to screen for value, momentum, and dividend stocks together. This screener is designed to pick winning value stocks that pay between 3% and 5% dividend yield, with reasonable market capitalizations, and are tradable with up to $100,000 in capital.

This basically combines the three screeners. The screen does fine over the last ten years and more than doubles the original investment. This screen also returns fewer than ten stocks, which is much easier to implement.[5] Finally, you might notice some flat lines in the backtest, such as mid-2009 to early 2010—these are periods where the screener does not return anything. You will have to hold cash (at a 0% return) during these periods.

In this case, before running the backtest, I also modified the rebalancing period to quarterly, instead of the default weekly. Recall that the rebalancing period determines how often the portfolio is refreshed and reweighted based on the screen's updated results. A quarterly rebalance means at the beginning of each quarter, you will run the screen, divide your money equally between all stocks that pass it, and then hold them until the end of the quarter. At the end of the quarter, you will cash out, rerun the screen, and divide the proceeds equally among all the new companies that pass the screen.

Realistically, no one will rebalance a portfolio weekly, and quarterly results will be more accurate. The easiest way to change the rebalancing period is by clicking on the Trading Rules tab, clicking on the Rebalance Weekly field under the Backtest Trading Rules section, and choosing Rebalance Quarterly.

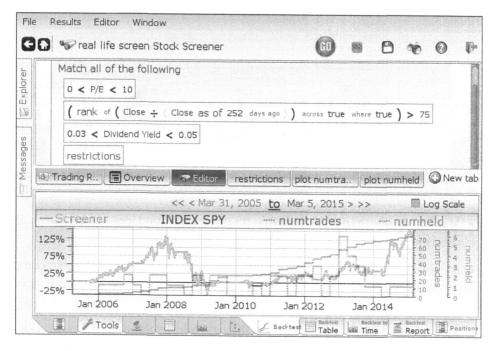

Figure 3.11 A real-life screener

However, the other important thing is the *restrictions* word in the Stock Screener editor. This invokes a set of restrictions in the next tab and is important enough to warrant a separate subsection. Ultimately, this is a more realistic screen.

The Restrictions Tab

You'll notice a tab titled Restrictions in the previous screens (see Figure 3.12). This is a tab I use to exclude all the stocks I do not want to even consider when deciding which quantitative measures to optimize. You don't have to call it restrictions. You can call it anything you want. I chose *restrictions* because it seems like an apt name for what I'm trying to do with the tab.

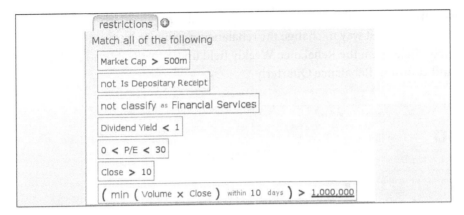

Figure 3.12 The Restrictions tab

I recommend this as standard practice for all serious screens.[6] In this case, I'm excluding stocks based on the following criteria:

- **Market cap less than $500 million**—It's generally a good idea to filter out smaller companies because these often have high transaction costs.

- **ADRs**—American Depository Receipts (or ADRs) are shares of foreign companies that trade in the United States. The financial data for these shares is sometimes inaccurate due to different accounting standards in different countries.

- **Financials**—I exclude these because they often have odd financial ratios (PB, in particular, is odd for financial companies) compared with companies in other industries.

- **Dividend yield**—This particular screen is a dividend yield screener. Dividend yield is computed as dividend paid over the last year divided by the share price. This is a sanity upper bound—a dividend yield of more than 100% means the stock paid more than its current trading price in dividends last year. Not a good sign. (In this case, this is redundant because my main screener also screens for this.)

- **0 < PE < 30**—Pick profitable companies that are not too expensive. This excludes companies that don't make money and those that are trading too expensive compared with what they make. (In this case, this is redundant because my main screener also screens for this.)[7]

- **Companies with a share price less than $10**—Penny stocks have some unconventional properties that I'd rather avoid.

- **Stocks that don't have $1 million minimum daily volume for the ten days prior to the rebalance**—If you're planning to trade these stocks, you should make sure they actually trade.

Creating multiproperty/operator expressions in Equities Lab can be a little tricky the first few times you do it.

(min (Volume × Close) within 10 days) > 1,000,000

To create multiproperty expressions like the one above, it is helpful to keep Equities Lab's parsing tree in mind. Equities Lab parses statements like this by breaking each statement by a "node" operator. For example, in the sample statement, the top "node" is the ">" sign. The next one is the "min" operator, and finally the "X" operator. Equities Lab computes expressions starting at the bottom node, and works up. So first, it evaluates "Volume X Close." Then, it evaluates the min of that within the last 10 days. Finally, it compares this number with the 1,000,000 and sees if the stock passes the screen.

To create an expression like this, start from the top node and work downward with the operators. So first, type in a ">" and press Enter. Two blanks will be created and you will be in the left blank. Then type "min..." and choose the "min-within" command and two more blanks will be created. Finally, in the first blank, type the "*" command and two more blanks will be created. Now you can fill in the blanks at your leisure. As you follow these steps, you should see the following sequence appear in the Editor.

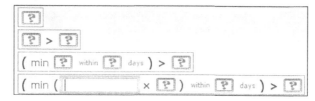

This is just one example of a set of restrictions you can use to guide your investments. You may have your own. For example, if you are morally opposed to smoking, you can exclude Tobacco companies with:

not classify as Tobacco Products

Once you have your exclusions, you can then pick whatever you want from the stocks that remain. In the previous case, I further screened for value, momentum, and dividend yield. However, you can use a Restrictions tab in any sort of screen. For example, if you are interested in the top 10% of dividend yield paying companies, you could have the screener eventually pick the top 10% of dividend payers that pass through the exclusion criteria by doing the following:

It is generally a good idea to filter based on exclusions before picking the stocks you want from what remains than to pick the stocks you want and then filter those. This is particularly true if you are picking based on a criterion that is correlated with exclusion criteria. You might end up with no stocks!

The Difference Exclusion Criteria Make

Just to highlight the importance of exclusions, Figures 3.13 and 3.14 compare the results of the real-life screener with and without restrictions.

Figure 3.13 Real-life screener with restrictions

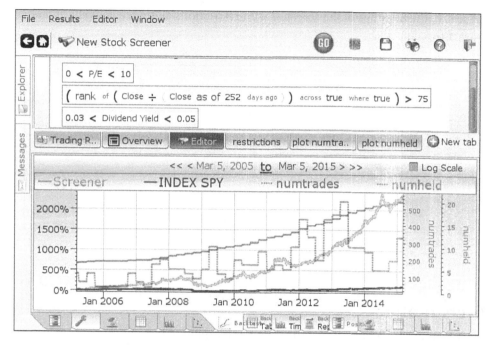

Figure 3.14 Real-life screener without restrictions

In this case, the performance without restrictions is many times greater than the performance with restrictions. In fact, even the number of holdings is quite tractable. However, I do not know how liquid the stocks are in the "without restrictions" version. Looking at the holdings, it is apparent that a number of these holdings have not traded today, as shown in Figure 3.15. Thus, although the backtest performance is good, it is unlikely to be replicable in real-life settings due to illiquidity.

Ticker	Company	Close	Market ...	Volume	Volume A...	Change...	Re
CIHKY	China Merch...	10.95	54.64b	5,255	2,849	-3.78%	0
MAC	Macerich	83.8	13.23b	2.05m	1.04m	-0.65%	0
BPY	Brookfield P...	24.97	6.09b	154,035	269,865	2.91%	0
MIC	Macquarie I...	78.99	5.6b	612,085	606,721	6.28%	0
CNGRY	Catlin Group	21.15	3.85b	0	954	-0.47%	0
PBF	PBF Energy	30.38	2.91b	656,433	1.7m	7.85%	0
HUIHY	Huabao Intl...	39.2	2.43b	0	47.33	-6.22%	0
SHZNY	Shenzhen E...	32.18	1.4b	0	0	0%	0
AEC	Associated ...	24.12	1.38b	186,594	405,961	-1.22%	0
DKL	Delek Logis...	41.31	1.01b	56,895	92,966	0.63%	0
CTMMB	CTM Media ...	160	147.7m	0	57.23	23.08%	0
MCEMB	Monarch Ce...	28.04	111.1m	0	0	0%	0
PSDI F	Prism Medical	8.17	68.8m	0	188.3	7.59%	0

Figure 3.15 Holdings without restrictions

In contrast, the holdings of the screener with restrictions all traded actively, as shown in Figure 3.16.

Ticker	Company	Close	Market ...	Volume	Volume A...	Change...	Ret
MAC	Macerich	83.8	13.23b	2.05m	1.04m	-0.65%	0
BPY	Brookfield P...	24.97	6.09b	154,035	269,865	2.91%	0
MIC	Macquarie I...	78.99	5.6b	612,085	606,721	6.28%	0
PBF	PBF Energy	30.38	2.91b	656,433	1.7m	7.85%	0
AEC	Associated ...	24.12	1.38b	186,594	405,961	-1.22%	0
DKL	Delek Logis...	41.31	1.01b	56,895	92,966	0.63%	0

Figure 3.16 Holdings with restrictions

Diversification

Diversification is the idea that spreading your capital across more stocks reduces the risk to each individual stock you own. It is important in quantitative strategies (and investing in general). The good news is it is easy to control the level of diversification by implementing screens slightly differently. For example, Figure 3.17 shows a simple value screen with restrictions that we were working with earlier.

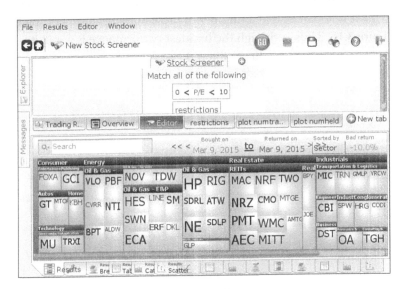

Figure 3.17 Value with restrictions

The restrictions are the standard ones discussed previously. You can see the screen is currently returning about 65 or so names. If you invested equally in each of these companies, you would have about 2% in each stock. This is quite diversified, but adding companies would increase diversification. Similarly, removing companies would reduce diversification. Diversification typically reduces the risk of the portfolio. If one of the companies crashes, a well-diversified portfolio with many holdings will be much less severely affected than a concentrated portfolio with fewer companies.

On the other hand, the more companies in your portfolio, the more you will trade, generating transaction costs. I consider transaction costs in detail in Chapter 8, "Rebalancing—Why, How, and How Often." However, as a simple illustration, implementing a portfolio with these 65 companies with a brokerage account that charges $10 per trade would cost $650. If, instead, you only had 10 companies, that would cost only $100 in commissions.

You can set screens to return a maximum number of holdings by clicking the Trading Rules tab and clicking the Add Max section in the Max Holdings panel. When you add a maximum number of holdings, Equities Lab directs you to enter how to order the list of stocks, so it can pick the "top 10." In Figure 3.18, I picked the top-10 stock by previous year returns, combining elements of momentum into the value screen.

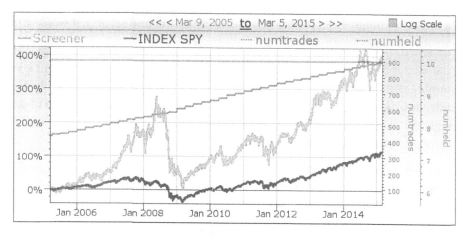

Figure 3.18 Limiting the number of holdings

In general, reducing holdings increases the standard deviation of the portfolio and other measures of risk. It also reduces transaction costs. Additionally, if your original screener returns a lot of stocks, reducing holdings strategically often increases the performance of the screener. The left set of performance characteristics shown in Table 3.2 are from the capped screener, and the right ones are from the full screener.[8] Capping the holdings strategically increased the performance but also increased the risk.

Table 3.2 Some Summary Statistics from the Results Summary Tab

Percentile	Returns (Monthly, Yield Adj.)	Percentile	Returns (Monthly, Yield Adj.)
Average	1.64%	Average	1.33%
Median	2.56%	Median	2.39%
Standard Deviation	7.66%	Standard Deviation	6.36%

Diversification across Industry, Market Cap, and So Forth

In addition to simply diversifying across more or fewer stocks, you might want to diversify across industries. Our real-life screener described earlier had an industry concentration problem. In particular, many of the returned stocks were in the real estate and oil and gas sectors. This is problematic because if you invest a majority of your capital in a single sector, and that sector suffers, you stand to lose a lot of money.

It is easy to develop a screen that limits the number of holdings per industry. Such a screen does two things: First, it sorts companies by sector, and second, it selects a subset of companies in each sector according to rules you specify.

The first step is to group companies by sector. This can be accomplished in two ways: by grouping companies by the first digit of their Standard Industrial Classification, or SIC code, or by grouping companies based on the Morningstar classification of sectors. Although the classification schemes are similar, they are not equivalent. Equities Lab enables you to work with either classification scheme.

Next, you will need to dictate the rules by which the holdings in each sector are chosen. To do this, you have to move away from the absolute filtering criteria you have been working under and move to relative filtering criteria.

The rank feature you saw briefly earlier is an example of a relative filtering criterion. The screen shown in Figure 3.19 no longer filters for a dividend yield between x% and y%. Instead, it chooses the top 20% of dividend payers across a range of industries among what is left after applying the restriction criterion.

Alternatively, you can use the position command to choose the top three dividend payers in each sector, as shown in Figure 3.20.

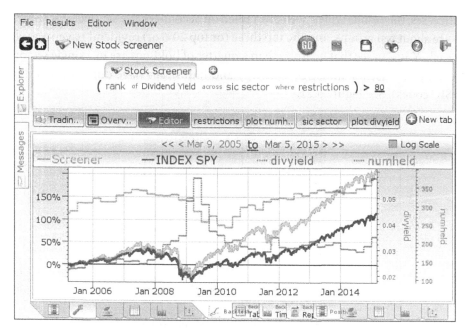

Figure 3.19 Picking top 20% of dividend payers by sector

Figure 3.20 Picking the top three dividend payers in each sector

---

In both cases, the results will be well diversified on account of the sic_sector screen. Thus, there are about ten groups, and the top three (or top 20% of) dividend payers are chosen from each. You can see that no more than a quarter of holdings are in a single sector (and that is only because the holdings in energy and industrials have different first digits of their SIC codes). See Figure 3.21.

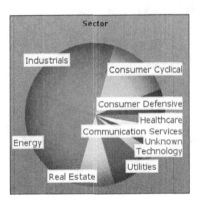

Figure 3.21 Breakout of sectors in a diversified screen

When you actually look at the holdings (Figure 3.22), you will see there is a fair amount of diversification across sectors, as identified by their SIC code. The diversification can also be done by "Morningstar Industry Code" or "Morningstar Sector Code." Simply put one of those terms into the Across field and that will be the category according to which the slices will be grouped.

Ticker	Company	Close	Market ...	Sector	Change...	divyield	F
AAPL	Apple	128.5	736.3b	Technology	8.51%	0.015	C
MSFT	Microsoft	43.05	353.7b	Technology	2.69%	0.027	C
JNJ	Johnson & J...	101.7	285b	Healthcare	-0.05%	0.027	C
WMT	Wal-Mart St...	82.58	269.4b	Consumer ...	-3.44%	0.023	C
GE	General Elec...	25.66	259.7b	Industrials	4.96%	0.035	C
PG	Procter & G...	84.35	228.5b	Consumer ...	-1.48%	0.03	C
PFE	Pfizer	34.64	210.3b	Healthcare	8.63%	0.031	C
VZ	Verizon Co...	49.07	203.3b	Communica...	3.17%	0.044	C
ORCL	Oracle	43.61	192.3b	Technology	1.61%	0.011	C
KO	Coca-Cola	42.5	185.1b	Consumer ...	1.89%	0.028	C
DIS	Walt Disney	105.6	176.9b	Consumer ...	6.19%	0.011	C
T	AT&T	34	176.5b	Communica...	-0.52%	0.053	C
IBM	IBM	159.4	159.3b	Technology	1.69%	0.027	C

Bought on << < Mar 9, 2015 to Mar 9, 2015 > >> Export

Figure 3.22 Holdings when picking top three dividend payers in each sector

Stocks that have paid out anything more than 10% of their stock price in dividends are likely to cut their dividends. However, there is also some chance that the stock price recovers if the dividend proves to be sustainable. Above 20% yields, however, it is almost guaranteed that the dividend will be cut. As testament to this, both Seadrill and Transocean, showing yield above or close to 20%, have cut dividends recently.

In general, the fundamental tension is risk versus reward. Diversification across sectors (or larger numbers) leads to a decrease in the backtest results/dividend yields/whatever else you are trying to maximize. Diversification also leads to reduced risk in the strategy. Where you choose to lie on this spectrum is entirely up to you—you can choose to put all your eggs in a single, very high-performing basket, or spread them around. The good news is that you can run the numbers both ways relatively painlessly and see which set of numbers appeals to you. In my case, I prefer more diversified portfolios by far, despite the sacrifice in performance.

Endnotes

1. As it turns out, momentum is used by the mutual fund industry and explains much of mutual fund performance persistence (Carhart, 1997).

2. The Across and Where fields are more interesting. Entering *true* simply says do this ranking for and across all stocks. You could also enter *industry* or *deciles of market cap* in Across—this would create the ranking by returns separately for each of these groups. If you enter *EPS > 0* in the Where field, the ranking will only be computed for stocks with positive EPS numbers.

3. In most academic papers, momentum is actually measured as returns from a year ago to a month ago. This is because there is some evidence that short-term momentum is mean reverting. That is, stocks that do well over the last month tend to go down next month (and vice versa). You can easily implement this flavor of momentum as well; simply change the first close in the formula to "close as of 21 days ago."

4. The dividend yield is simply the dividends paid over the last 12 months, divided by the stock price. This yield for the overall market is about 2%.

5. plot_numheld plots the field "Number of Holdings," which varies between 0 and 6; plot_numtrades plots the field "Number of Trades," which ends up being a total of 80 over the period.

6. Equities Lab actually has a base level set of restrictions in place. This is very basic and simply excludes companies with Market Cap < $50 million and trading price less than a dollar. If you want to explore these micro cap penny stocks in Equities Lab, you can remove these built-in restrictions by creating a tab called "universe" and setting a single file in it to be "true."

7. Equities Lab codes companies with negative earnings as having undefined PE ratios. This will ensure they do not enter the screen.

8. These statistics are available in the Backtest Report tab, along with a number of other useful statistics regarding the backtest. For more details on what these are, see Chapter 7, "How to Measure Performance."

4

For the Deeper Divers among Us: How to Use Quantitative Strategies to Enhance Fundamental Valuations

As opposed to the quantitative investor, most successful stock pickers invest after doing a complete analysis (or "deep dive") of a company. Although accounting ratios and PE type valuation ratios may be part of their decision-making process, they will often know as much (or more) about the companies they invest in as senior management.

Although quantitative investing tools cannot help investors find out much about a company's business, they can still be useful to such investors. In particular, they can help these investors narrow down the list of companies they have to review in their deep fundamental analysis. If the job of fundamental analysts is likened to looking for the one significantly undervalued needle in a haystack, quantitative tools can point to the one or two handfuls of hay in the stack where the needle is most likely to be. This is a huge boon for fundamental analysts, as their most precious commodity is time, and spending time on only the highest quality ideas is absolutely necessary to maximize the returns they generate.

Explaining techniques for doing a deep dive fundamental valuation on a company is, unfortunately, beyond the scope of this book. Instead, this chapter focuses on explaining how quantitative tools can be useful to these investors by describing two case studies of how fundamental investors used quantitative methods to improve their investing outcomes.

Case Study #1: Helping Dad

Here is an example of a case where I developed a screener to help my father invest 50k–100k. My father is not by nature a quantitative investor. He was an engineer by training and rose to upper-middle management ranks at a tech company in Asia. He understands business, and would prefer to understand the business of a company he invests in rather than blindly toss his money into a "system."

The screener I developed for him has several purposes:

- I want to generate dividends.

- I want to find value stocks.

- I want stocks my father has heard of, or at least can do research on.

- I want to make sure any stocks he chooses from the list is sufficiently liquid to support 10k–20k being invested in them.

- I want a list of about 30 to 40 stocks to give my father from which he can start doing analysis on individual names.

I started off with a screen that is fairly similar to the value and yield screens described in Chapter 3, "Creating a Screen—The Nuts and Bolts of Choosing a Quantitative Investing Strategy," as shown in Figure 4.1. I tightened up the market capitalization restriction to only include companies with a market capitalization above $5 billion. This ensures my father will be able to obtain news and research reports for such companies relatively easily.

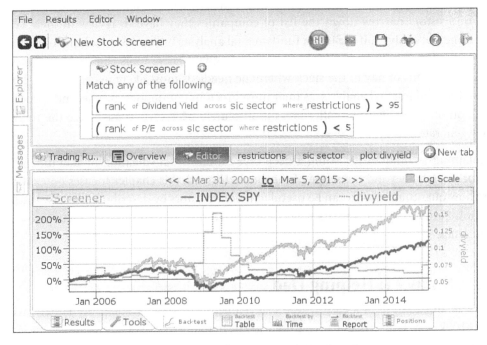

Figure 4.1 Backtest of screener to support deep dive

The default way Equities Lab treats multiple criteria is it tries to match all of them. To switch from `Match all of the following` to `Match any of the following`, simply click on the area and type in "or" (to switch back, do the same and type in "and").

The backtest results look promising, and the dividend yield hovers around a healthy 5% level. This is important as my father has retired, and the dividend will generate a stream of income off of his capital so he can pay the bills.

Also note that rather than diversify across industries, the screen simply picks the 5% of dividend payers that pass the restriction screen and the top 5% of value stocks (that is, those with the lowest 5% of PE ratios). This is because I don't particularly care about giving a diversified list to my father. He knows his portfolio and will pick stocks off the list that will complement whatever holdings he has. I chose the 5% level because that is what matched the number of stocks I wanted. If I wanted to give more names in the list, I could relax the screen to choose the top 10% of dividend payers and value stocks that pass the restriction.

The final list I sent is shown in Figure 4.2.

Ticker	Company	Close	Market ...	Change...	divyield	P/E	Re
NKE	Nike	97.52	83.91b	5.59%	0.011	28.95	0
FOXA	Twenty-Firs...	34.97	74.14b	1.91%	0.007	8.31	0
DD	E I du Pont ...	78.12	70.49b	6.87%	0.024	19.96	0
SBUX	Starbucks	93.06	70.1b	6%	0.012	28.34	0
F	Ford Motor	16.03	63.73b	2.62%	0.032	20.74	0
HPO	Hewlett-Pac...	34.19	62.53b	-8.85%	0.018	13.29	0
MDLZ	Mondelez In...	36.44	60.74b	1.7%	0.016	28.86	0
ACN	Accenture	90.91	59b	2.39%	0.022	20.51	0
CNI	Canadian N...	68.96	55.93b	0.31%	0.013	24.22	0
TMO	Thermo Fis...	128.9	51.58b	2.74%	0.005	27.6	0
TJX	TJX Compa...	68.29	47.29b	1.37%	0.01	22.67	0
GD	General Dy...	136.2	45.32b	-1.83%	0.018	17.72	0
LYB	LyondellBas...	87.24	40.99b	1.45%	0.033	10.74	0
SO	Southern	44.83	40.51b	-11.77%	0.046	19.58	0
EMR	Emerson El...	57.78	39.69b	-2.32%	0.031	18.36	0
KMB	Kimberly-Cl...	108.4	39.64b	-1.57%	0.031	28.05	0
ITW	Illinois Tool ...	98.2	37.51b	2.23%	0.018	21.17	0

(Bought on Mar 9, 2015 to Returned on Mar 9, 2015 — Export)

Figure 4.2 Final short list sent—with data on stocks to help selection for deep analysis

Some of the companies on the list were familiar to my father (and are probably familiar to you). The first thing my father did was to explore the names he had not heard of. In particular, he focused on non-energy names. After he understood what each of those companies did and confirmed the profitability and dividend stability of those companies, he chose seven of the companies from the list and invested $10k in each one.

Case Study #2: Integrating with a Fundamental Fund [Exact Details Changed to Maintain Confidentiality]

A fundamentally oriented fund was interested in adding a quantitative outlook to its repertoire. However, rather than simply start a quantitative fund housed under the overall umbrella, the fund decided to use screens to enhance the existing fundamental business.

The fund manager decided on a list of six screens that he liked. These were as follows:

- A value screen

- A momentum screen

- A dividend yield screen

- A low volatility screen

- A low beta screen

- An F score screen

The fund checked each investment that it was invested in or was considering investing in to see how many of these screens it passed. That number was called its *quant* score.

As time went by, the performance of both actual investments and those that were considered, but passed, was linked to their quant score. When it became clear that passed investments with a quant score of 3 or more were actually outperforming actual investments with a quant score of 1 or 0, the fund very quickly implemented a rule that the quant score would be factored into the decision-making process. Specifically, the investment universe was restricted to companies with a quant score of 2 and above. Additionally, the case for passing companies with a quant score of 4, 5, or 6 would have to be very strong. Finally, higher quant score companies were given higher weights in the portfolio.

This systematic process of including quantitative investing elements in a fundamentally driven investment process improved the discipline of the fund's investment process. Additionally, restricting the universe of stocks to those passing a quant screen increased the likelihood of finding high upside stocks that had good quantitative fundamentals.

Overall Thoughts on Merging Deep Stock Analysis and Quantitative Techniques

There are numerous ways to merge quantitative investing with deep dives. The first case study involved using quantitative tools to screen for companies, and then doing in-depth analysis on selected names from the screen. The latter simply created a score to evaluate the quantitative appeal of a given investment. These are two of many ways to combine the two techniques. Ultimately, quantitative tools should serve to enhance fundamental investment. Regardless of how you choose to use quantitative tools in your fundamental investing agenda, I urge you to keep a record of how quantitative techniques affected your investment performance. Like the fund that kept a quant score in parallel while still maintaining its original in-depth analysis, you will be able to compute how much (if any) value a quantitative tilt would add to your investments. If you find a significant performance boost, you can simply start to incorporate the quantitative input into your decision making.

Finally, a word of warning: Stock picking through fundamental analysis is a subjective process despite the effort analysts put in to make the process as objective as possible. This means that it is subject to all the behavioral biases that can be avoided by pursuing a purely quantitative agenda (see Chapter 13, "Behavioral Biases Avoided by Investing Quantitatively"). This means that simply using quantitative techniques to guide your investments will not spare you from the effects of these biases, and you should be cognizant of them in your investments.

5

Market Timing—Getting In and Out at the Right Time

In addition to filtering securities to invest in at any given time, quantitative strategies can also provide guidance on timing decisions. In particular, if I were to believe that markets revert, I may set a strategy up to invest in stocks after a year of bad performance, and invest in cash after a year of good performance.

A number of quantitative trading strategies actually focus on this aspect of quantitative analysis. Technical analysis, for example, is nothing but a timing screen based on historical stock prices for a single stock. However, technical analysis is generally done by eyeballing charts, and proponents will often say there's an "art" to the process, rather than simply a set formula. For more information, see Chapter 6, "Technical Analysis for Quants."

The other investors who love timing screens are macro investors. *Macro* is a broad term, describing investors who take cues from macroeconomic variables to guide their trades. Famous macro investors include legendary fund managers like George Soros and John Paulson.[1] Macro investors will not exclusively use a timing screen to trade, but will rather look at signals coming from various macro factors, subjectively synthesize them along with recent news, and then execute a trade.

This chapter describes two timing screens. The first is a value timing screen that relies on average PE levels. You often hear the phrase that the "stock market is overvalued." That typically refers to the price of stocks being high relative to some measure of earnings.[2] The second is a more macro screen, relying on unemployment indicators. Finally, this chapter concludes with a warning on overfitting.

Market Timing Based on Value

Keeping with the value theme from previous chapters, one might hypothesize that holding stocks when PE ratios for the market as a whole are low and holding cash when they are high is a winning strategy. The idea is exactly the same as before: Buying earnings for cheap is likely to be profitable.

You can test this hypothesis by using Equities Lab. First, you have to measure the average level of the PE over time, across the set of stocks in which you are interested in investing. For this example, I will do this for the stocks in my restrictions set. The main innovation in market timing screens is the use of a macro variable, such as the PE ratio of all stocks in my screen, or the unemployment level, or something else. The variable is tracked over time regardless of what is in my portfolio. You can create such a variable in Equities Lab by plotting it, and putting an underscore (the "_" symbol) at the end of the variable name to indicate it is a macro variable.[3] I do this by creating a tab that looks like the one shown in Figure 5.1.

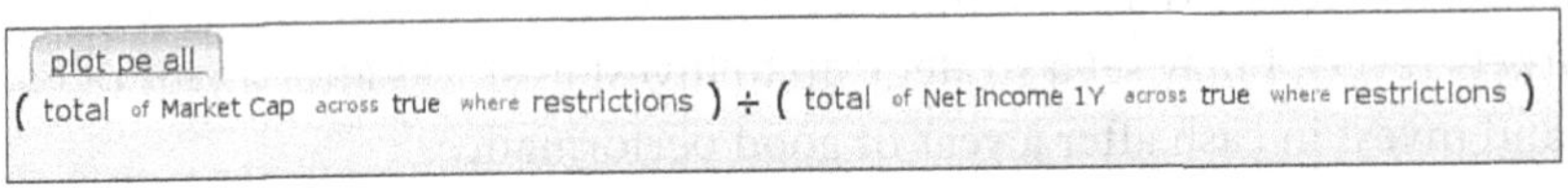

plot pe all
(total of Market Cap across true where restrictions) ÷ (total of Net Income 1Y across true where restrictions)

Figure 5.1 Plotting PE of the universe

This adds up the market cap for all companies in my restrictions set, divides it by the trailing 12 months' net income of all these companies, and stores it in a variable called "pe_all_." Note that simply taking the average of the PEs of these companies is not a good idea because some of them might have very high PEs, which would skew the average above what it should be. [4]

You can then use the "then-since" command to create your trading rule. You want to move into stocks when the average PE level drops below 17 and move out of stocks when the PE level climbs above 20.

You can do this by implementing the screen shown in Figure 5.2.

Note that in this screen, you have to set the screen to match *any* of the conditions. (Click on Match All of the Following and type in "or." This turns it into "Match Any of the Following.") As you can see, the screen is in stocks when the PE is low, and stays out when the PE increases. The screen is unimpressive, underperforming the market severely. Thus, it seems that timing screens based on trailing PEs does not do much for performance.

In fact, most timing screens based on PEs use forward-looking PE measures or PE ratios where earnings are averaged over a longer period than a single year. Unfortunately, estimate data is not included in the current version of Equities Lab, and if you want to test whether this works, you must gather data yourself. To compute data using earnings over multiple years, you can simply take the sum of net income numbers from past years and take an average.

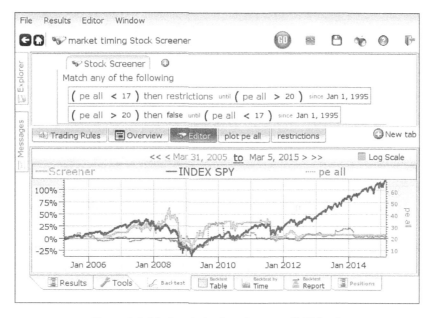

Figure 5.2 Market timing based on overall PE levels

Other Market Timing Strategies, or the Wonder of Quandl Data

In addition to simply screening for value in the overall market, there is also a wealth of publicly available data to use in timing strategies. The best repository of this data is in Quandl. According to their Web site, Quandl "sources data from central banks, exchanges, brokers, statistical agencies, think-tanks, academics, and private companies. There are almost 500 high quality data sources at your fingertips at Quandl.com." They basically aggregate freely available data in a convenient, single destination. They do have some premium data series, but there's also a lot of free data series to work with.[5]

To use Quandl data in your screens, go to Quandl and search for what you are interested in. As an example, Figure 5.3 shows what unemployment data looks like.

Note the Permalink on the lower left of the page. Copy that link and paste it into a variable in Equities Lab. For example, I'm creating a tab, "plot_unemp_" and have the unemployment permalink in it.[6]

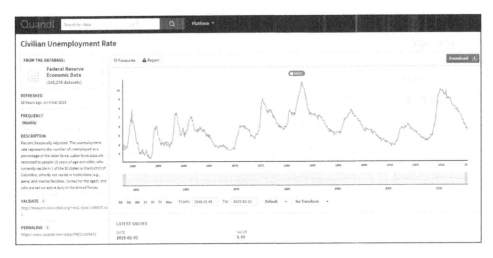

Figure 5.3 Unemployment data from Quandl (www.quandl.com)

Now, I will have a screen that holds high beta stocks if the unemployment rate has fallen or stayed the same over two quarters and low beta stocks otherwise. Figure 5.4 shows how this performs.

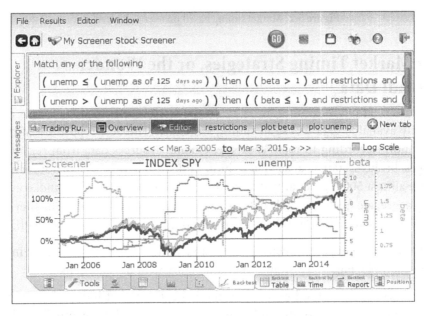

Figure 5.4 Unemployment timing screen (with forward-looking bias)

You can see that it somewhat outperforms over the last ten years, but again, nothing impressive. One thing to note here is that the unemployment series ends in December 2014 despite the fact that it is currently March 2015 as of this writing. This is because unemployment data is typically released with a lag. This has to be factored into screens. Equities Lab does not automatically lag variables, so our current screen has a bit of forward-looking bias in it, as we are filtering based on unemployment numbers that may not be out at the time of filtering. A more accurate way to execute this screen would probably be to lag all unemployment numbers by an added one month or one quarter (see Figure 5.5).

Figure 5.5 Unemployment macro screen (with trading conditions broken into multiple lines to fit on the page)

This lags all unemployment numbers by one quarter. The backtest results are shown in Figure 5.6 and are similar (and in fact slightly better).

Figure 5.6 Unemployment macro screen (no forward-looking bias)

Recall that one quarter is roughly 63 trading days. Thus, this screen is in high beta stocks if the unemployment rate one quarter ago is lower or the same as the unemployment rate from three quarters ago. This avoids any look-ahead bias because the unemployment rate one quarter ago would definitely be available at the time of filtering. The screen does slightly better, but it is still nothing impressive.

However, after looking at the results, perhaps you notice that the inflexion points of unemployment (that is, the points at which it stopped going down and started going up in 2007) signaled the beginning of the financial crisis of 2008. You think to yourself, "Perhaps a timing screen that sells off and refrains from purchasing stocks for a year after such an inflexion point would be a good screen."

You have just fallen prey to the curse of foreknowledge. The following section discusses why doing this is a bad idea and why it is particularly tempting to do this for timing screens.

Why Market Timing Strategies Are Easier to Overfit Than Stock Screening Strategies

Timing screens often have a single input signal. In the case of the previous screen, it was the unemployment rate that was the signal. This contrasts with stock screeners, which have multiple inputs (for example, PE, market cap, momentum, dividend yield) generating a different signal for every stock. When you have a single signal, and you know what happens to the market (or a stock price) over the course of a backtest, it becomes very easy to propose rules based on that one signal that will take advantage of market upturns and avoid market downturns.

Consider the preceding example, where you notice the inflexion point right before the plummeting of the stock market right before a *known* market downturn. In this case, not only do you know exactly when to exit, but because of the curse of fore knowledge, you also know to stay out for exactly a year. A backtest based on these rules would definitely outperform in this sample but is unlikely to do so going forward.

This is a form of overfitting and doing this will not lead to sustainable outperformance. It is very similar to the example where we invested in stocks like Apple, and backtests looked great because we were including Apple in them! In this case, too, we know what is going to happen, and if we are not intellectually honest with ourselves in creating timing screens, we will fall prey to this sort of overfitting very easily.

Endnotes

1. George Soros has made billions betting on currencies, emerging markets, and various other themes. During the Asian crisis of 1997, he was accused of tanking the Malaysian economy through his currency trades. Paulson made $5 billion off of shorting the subprime market during the financial crisis of 2008.

2. The absolute level of a stock market index does not have much meaning, without comparing it with earnings, or past levels. Comparing it with past levels may also be tricky because the earnings may have increased or decreased.

3. The underscore ensures that this variable is plotted on a daily level. Most screener-specific variables are computed once at the beginning of each rebalance period and stay constant through the rebalance period. This saves immensely on computing time. Putting the underscore after the variable name forces Equities Lab to compute the variable at a daily level so you can observe what it does in between rebalances.

4. The average of two companies' PEs is not the same as the PE computed using the sum of the two companies' market caps and incomes. For example, if company A has a market cap of 100 and earnings of 1 (for a PE of 100), and company B has a market cap of 100 and earnings of 10, for a PE of 10, the average PE is 55, whereas the PE using the sums of the market caps and incomes is a more reasonable 18.2 (computed as (100+100)/(10+1)).

5. From Quandl's Web site, "We're zealous supporters of open data. We believe information should be free. Quandl will eventually offer premium data features and data on this site, but we will never compromise on one core principle: If we can get the data for free then you get the data for free."

6. The _ after the "plot_unemp" statement forces Equities Lab to refresh this variable at a daily level. Most variables are refreshed at the rebalancing points. Because unemployment is a macro variable, and I might be rebalancing as little as quarterly or annually, it is important for me to get the data in between the rebalances correct as well.

6

Technical Analysis for Quants

Technical analysis is a specific form of a timing screen. Technical analysis is the science (or art) of reading stock price charts and predicting what will happen next. Figure 6.1 shows an example of technical analysis from the Wikipedia entry on the subject.

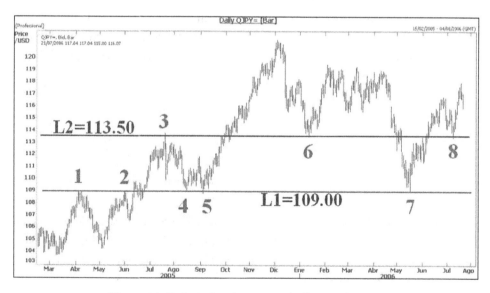

Figure 6.1 Technical analysis example (from Wikipedia)

This chart plots the price of the Japanese Yen against the U.S. dollar. The Wikipedia caption to the chart states, "Stock chart showing levels of support (4, 5, 6, 7, and 8) and resistance (1, 2, and 3); levels of resistance tend to become levels of support and vice versa." The idea behind this piece of technical analysis is that initially, the lower line is a level of resistance (or a historical maximum reached at point 1). Once that is broken, at point 2, the price is likely to continue rising. It does so until point 3, at which point it falls, creating a new level of resistance. The old level of resistance is now a level of support, and the prediction is that the price should fall no further than that point (points 4 and 5). So after point 5, the price breaks the old level of resistance (unmarked) and surges up.

In any case, rather than focus on the mechanics of this exact chart, I want to highlight the idea behind technical analysis that past prices have some predictive power on future prices. Of course, it is easier to look at a price chart and draw in these levels with all future information. It is harder, with these levels, to predict what happens next. So, for example, at the end of this chart, will the price increase? Will it decrease? Or does technical analysis not have a strong view?

In any case, it is easy to test whether a given technical indicator actually passes the test of time by performing a backtest on it.

Creating a Technical Screener

The easiest way to replicate a technical trading strategy is to do it for a single stock. In Equities Lab, you can do this with the Trading Model. Click on the Explorer tab on the left side and then click on the Trading Model button on the right. See Figure 6.2.

Figure 6.2 Creating a trading model

The Trading Model allows you to test trading rules on the purchase and sale of a single ticker. In this case, you're going to test a rule that buys a stock when it is above its one-month maximum price as of a week ago (that is, it is "breaking out") and then sells once it falls 5% below its monthly high.

The first thing you have to set is what security you are buying and what you are doing with your money when you are not investing it in the security.

As an example, Figure 6.3 shows that the security being trading is set as GE and the alternative security is set as cash. You can then use the Buy and Sell tabs to set the conditions for when to buy the stock and until when to hold it. See Figures 6.4 and 6.5.

Figure 6.3 Trading Model home screen

Figure 6.4 Technical trading buying rule

Sell GE after Close < ((max Close within 21 days) × 0.95)

Figure 6.5 Technical trading selling rule

After clicking Go, you can see this does slightly better than simply holding GE over ten years, but does not outperform the market, as shown in Figure 6.6. In fact, it actually loses a bit of money. The dark shaded portions of the chart are periods during which you are holding GE, and the non-shaded portions of the chart are periods during which you are holding cash.

Of course, this only looks at a single trading strategy for a single stock. You can switch symbols around to see if you generate similar results.

More generally, you can also use the stock screener to analyze what would happen if you ran this generally for a group of stocks, as shown in Figure 6.7.

The command used in Figure 6.7 is the "then-until-since" command. The "buy" condition is in the first term, the second term is simply what to buy (in this case it's "true," referring to all stocks), and the "until" term is the "sell" term. The second condition restricts running this screener to companies above the $5 billion market cap.

Running a ten-year backtest yields the results shown in Figure 6.8.

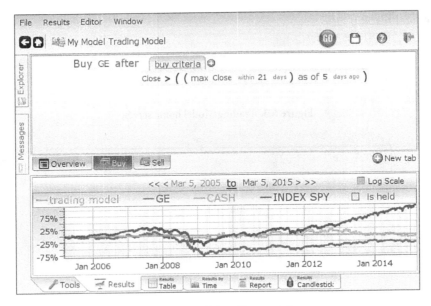

Figure 6.6 GM trading model

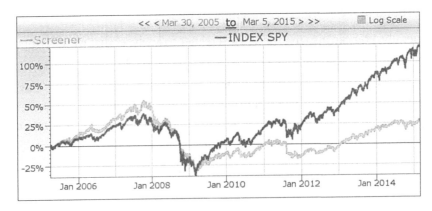

Figure 6.7 Backtesting a technical trading rule for all stocks

Figure 6.8 Running a technical screen for all stocks in the market

Of course, you can see that over a larger sample, this strategy isn't that great. It makes money, but severely lags the market. Of course, the strategy was not performing particularly well for GE to begin with, so maybe this is to be expected.

However, this process highlights some of the problems with technical analysis. Whatever rule you come up with to fit a given stock chart is:

- Often difficult to formulate in an algorithmic manner

- Often overfitted to the given stock chart

- Often does not work for other stocks

That being said, a lot of proponents of technical analysis simply respond with the argument that technical analysis is more of an art than a science, and each stock is different. This may indeed be the case, but then it is difficult to call technical trading strategies "quantitative" strategies. If the analyst is making human judgments on the strategy as it unfolds, it is subject to the same human biases that normal, nonquantitative strategies are. Additionally, if such strategies require constant human intervention, there is no way to code the strategy to have a computer run it.

Fragility

Fragility, or the lack of robustness, is one of the other main problems with technical analysis. Imagine you find a wonderful technical screen (such as the formula shown in Figure 6.9).

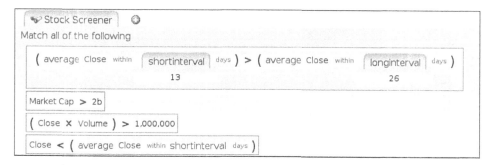

Figure 6.9 Technical screen example

What does this say? Merely that you (among your subset of companies you deem as "liquid") want the ones that have been going up in the medium term (13-day moving average is greater than the 26-day moving average), but that have been going down in the short term (closing price is less than the 13-day moving average). This yielded 20% annual performance over the last four years. What about going further back? See Figure 6.10.

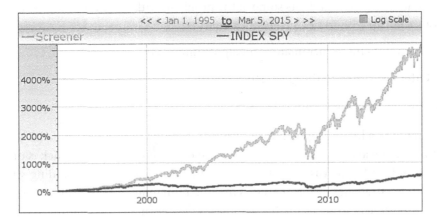

Figure 6.10 Technical screen backtest

Wow! 50x returns (or making fifty times your original investment) over 20 years would make you a millionaire in no time!

TIP

With such large returns, it is often useful to see things in log scale. Otherwise, we give too much weight, visually, to the spike at the end.

But here's the thing: This strategy doesn't care whether these companies earned more than last year, or whether they earned anything at all! The strategy also doesn't care what industries these companies landed in. Furthermore, it's not entirely internally consistent. "Buy companies that are taking a breather, over the long run?" It barely makes sense. What happens if you make a small change to the screen? Let's first change from using the closing price to the opening price. Figure 6.11 shows this backtest.

Figure 6.11 Technical screen open instead of close

Yes, this still outperforms, but it only generates 17x, rather than the 50x from earlier. The only difference was choosing the price at the beginning of the day versus the one at the end of the day. And if you change the parameters, for example, to 15 days and 30 days, your performance falls to 15x, using closing prices, as shown in Figure 6.12.

Figure 6.12 Technical analysis 15/30 versus 13/26

This is what I mean by fragility. Keeping the basic idea behind a screen the same and changing the numbers a bit should not change the backtest performance by these magnitudes. These magnitudes might not seem that important, as they both outperform the S&P 500 index fund handily. However, when you factor trading costs into the equation (these examples use 0.2% per trade), you find the charts shown in Figures 6.13 and 6.14, for the weekly screens.

Figure 6.13 Same conditions, with 0.2% commission costs; annual performance of about 14%

Figure 6.14 Same screener, using 15 and 30 days, (not 13 and 26 days); also with 0.2% commissions; annual performance of 1.68%

The charts speak for themselves. Simply changing the screen slightly by changing the "short" and "long" interval essentially "breaks" the screen.

Incidentally, fragility is not as much of a problem for screeners based on fundamental criteria. For example, if you were running a value screen, picking the bottom 10% of PE ratios or the bottom 15% of PE ratios would both work. One might work slightly better than the other, but they would both work.

Overall, the technical analysis backtest charts speak for themselves in portraying somewhat inconsistent trends that persist in frustrating technical analysts. My general sense is that it is difficult to systematically implement a quantitative trading strategy based on technical indicators. An exception to this rule is momentum, which was covered in Chapter 3, "Creating a Screen—The Nuts and Bolts of Choosing a Quantitative Investing Strategy," and is revisited in the following section.

Momentum—The One Exception to Skepticism Regarding Technical Analysis

This section returns to one of the screeners covered earlier in the book, and possibly the only technical indicator with a wealth of academic literature surrounding it: momentum. Recall that *momentum,* broadly defined, is the idea that winners continue to be winners, and losers continue to be losers. Figures 6.15 and 6.16 present two backtests. Look at the following charts and guess which one is which: One of the charts shows the backtest of investing in the worst 20% performing stocks over the last six months, and the other shows the backtest of investing in the best performing 20%. Both start in 1997, and rebalance yearly.

Figure 6.15 Either top or bottom 20% of performers over last 6 months

Figure 6.16 Either top or bottom 20% of performers over last 6 months

Of course, Figure 6.16 was the set of stocks that underperformed over the last six months. You probably guessed correctly, given what you know about momentum from Chapter 3. The fact that you know this tells you that there is information in the historical price charts—just not as much information as the proponents of technical analysis would have you believe.

Note that the fragility discussed in the previous section does not appear to be a major problem here—regardless of whether you use momentum over the last 3, 6, 9, or 12 months, you generate similar results. In fact, the only cases where momentum appears to go the other way is for very short periods, such as a day, a week, or a month. Short-term winners and losers tend to mean revert. (See Figure 6.17, it's much easier to follow in color.[1])Academic studies argue this is due to overreaction, although some studies also argue that trading at these "high" frequencies would incur transaction costs large enough to erase any potential gains. See Kang, Liu, and Ni (2002) and Conrad, Gultekin, and Kaul (1997) for examples.

A similar trend is there for under-performers. Regardless of the horizon of the underperformance, it persists. Only a very short term underperformance (days, weeks, or a month) is followed by a bounceback.

Thus, the fragility of technical analysis based strategies does not appear to be a problem for momentum. Winners continue to outperform and losers continue to lag.

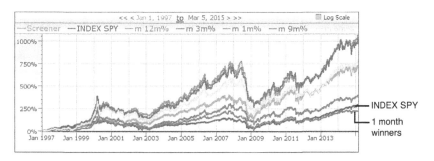

Figure 6.17 Varying momentum computation horizon—top 20% winners

Endnotes

1. The Screener line is Market Cap > 1B and reasonable trading volume. It's just above the faint line in the first chart, and just below the faint line in the second chart. The fact that the Screener line outperforms the S&P 500 over the period is just the size premium at work. (See the table of contents at the beginning of this book for directions on accessing this figure in color.)

7

How to Measure Performance

o far, most of the backtests in this book have focused on returns. This is the most obvious (and easiest) performance measure. It is intuitive, as cumulative returns represent what an investment will grow to in dollar terms.

However, you could potentially make a number of improvements to this measure. For example, simply measuring returns does not consider the risk involved in a strategy. Consider the two following strategies shown in Figure 7.1: safe and risky.

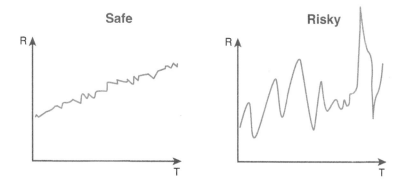

Figure 7.1 Safe versus risky strategies that make the same returns

These graphs show the cumulative returns (R) over time (T) for the two strategies. Although $100 invested in both these strategies would have ended up with roughly the same return over the period, the investor in the "Safe" strategy would be relaxed and sleeping well, whereas the investor in the "Risky" strategy would probably have had multiple coronaries during the period.

Although risk is the major component of performance not captured by using raw returns,[1] there are other adjustments to performance measurement discussed in this chapter.

Benchmarks

The main adjustment to performance begins with a question: What should I be comparing the returns from my screen against? The two easy answers are: (1) the overall market, most often represented by the S&P 500 (the default benchmark in Equities Lab) and (2) the risk-free rate.

What else could you compare returns against? There is no shortage of indices reflecting various investment strategies. For example, the Barclays Aggregate Bond Index (which was formerly called the Lehman Aggregate before Lehman's failure) reflects returns to a basket of bonds. These are available at http://index.barcap.com/. Figure 7.2 shows a screenshot as of this writing. If you have a portfolio of equities trying to compete with bonds, you might want to use one of these indices as a benchmark.

In general, pick the most "honest" index as a benchmark, but be sure to also compute and understand the raw returns.[2] Beating the S&P by 20% in a year where the S&P loses 40% is great, but you're still losing money!

U.S. and Canadian Indices									As of 17-Oct-2014
Index	Mod. Adj. Duration	Yield-to-Worst	1-day%	mtd%	ytd%	12-mth%	Currency	Return Type	Index Value
U.S. Universal	5.45	2.57	-0.00	1.27	5.48	5.08	USD	Unhedged	501.09
U.S. Aggregate	5.58	2.14	-0.10	1.46	5.61	4.94	USD	Unhedged	1,908.51
U.S. Aggregate Float Adjusted	5.65	2.07	-0.11	1.47	5.55	4.94	USD	Unhedged	129.18
U.S. Treasury	5.49	1.27	-0.21	1.57	4.68	3.62	USD	Unhedged	2,101.85
U.S. Treasury: 1-3 Year	1.95	0.43	-0.06	0.43	0.87	0.89	USD	Unhedged	253.01
U.S. Treasury: 3-5 Year	3.89	1.19	-0.17	1.38	2.61	1.97	USD	Unhedged	335.49
U.S. Treasury 3-7 Yr	4.62	1.40	-0.22	1.66	3.57	2.52	USD	Unhedged	353.34
U.S. Treasury: 5-7 Year	5.66	1.69	-0.29	2.07	5.08	3.32	USD	Unhedged	389.17
U.S. Treasury: 7-10 Year	7.88	2.07	-0.35	2.64	8.49	5.91	USD	Unhedged	429.18
U.S. Treasury: 10-20 Year	10.07	2.42	-0.40	3.07	12.61	9.22	USD	Unhedged	521.43
U.S. Treasury: 20+ Year	18.34	2.91	-0.56	4.55	21.89	17.03	USD	Unhedged	600.37
Short Treasury	0.46	0.07	-0.01	-0.00	0.10	0.12	USD	Unhedged	259.47
U.S. Treasury: U.S. TIPS	6.30	1.96	-0.07	1.78	5.51	3.17	USD	Unhedged	284.00
U.S. Credit	7.07	2.81	-0.05	1.73	7.50	7.39	USD	Unhedged	2,571.33
1-3 Yr Credit	1.98	1.03	-0.04	0.43	1.43	1.73	USD	Unhedged	1,497.14
U.S. Intermediate Credit	4.32	2.14	-0.08	1.19	4.57	4.56	USD	Unhedged	2,464.82
U.S. Long Credit A	13.96	4.22	-0.12	3.23	14.80	14.33	USD	Unhedged	3,202.35
U.S. Government/Credit	6.07	1.93	-0.14	1.61	5.80	5.16	USD	Unhedged	2,183.67
Intermediate U.S. Government/Credit	3.91	1.45	-0.13	1.16	3.41	3.00	USD	Unhedged	1,974.74
U.S. Mortgage Backed Securities	4.57	2.65	-0.00	1.12	5.39	4.57	USD	Unhedged	1,956.36
U.S. Corporate High Yield	4.35	6.13	1.08	0.15	3.65	5.87	USD	Unhedged	1,639.95
Municipal Bond	6.29	1.99	-0.21	1.25	8.92	9.67	USD	Unhedged	1,067.83
Barclays-Russell LDI 6 Year Index	5.89	2.25	0.11	1.54	5.96	5.72	USD	Unhedged	174.85
Barclays-Russell LDI 8 Year Index	7.83	2.85	-0.14	2.05	8.49	8.04	USD	Unhedged	187.69
Barclays-Russell LDI 10 Year Index	10.36	3.52	-0.14	2.57	11.80	11.18	USD	Unhedged	199.88
Barclays-Russell LDI 12 Year Index	12.18	3.88	-0.12	2.90	13.73	12.98	USD	Unhedged	207.16
Barclays-Russell LDI 14 Year Index	14.13	4.19	-0.11	3.23	15.54	14.93	USD	Unhedged	214.83
Barclays-Russell LDI 16 Year Index	16.51	4.57	0.04	3.58	17.42	16.86	USD	Unhedged	247.85

Figure 7.2 U.S. bond indices from http://index.barcap.com/

Standard Deviation

The standard deviation of returns is the most popular measure of risk. Basically, *standard deviation* is a measure of the average difference of all returns from the average return.[3] The easiest way to calculate it for a backtest is by exporting raw backtest data to a spreadsheet program such as Excel (see Video 7.1 and Figure 7.3) and then computing standard deviations in the spreadsheet.[4]

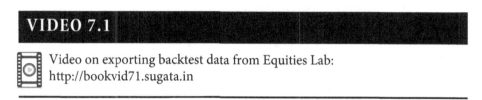

Video on exporting backtest data from Equities Lab:
http://bookvid71.sugata.in

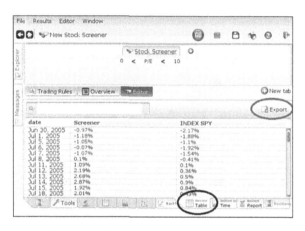

Figure 7.3 Exporting backtest data to Excel

So first, you need to open the results Table tab. This is simply the raw data that is used for creating the backtest charts. For example, the screened stocks returned –0.97% on June 30, 2005 and by July 18, 2005, the cumulative return on the strategy (stocks with PE between 0 and 10) had hit 2.01%. Export this data to a file by clicking the Export button (circled in the figure).

You should see a dialog box like the one shown in Figure 7.4. Simply choose the directory in which to save your spreadsheet, type in a name, and click Export. Then, open the file in Excel. You should see something similar to what is shown in Figure 7.5.

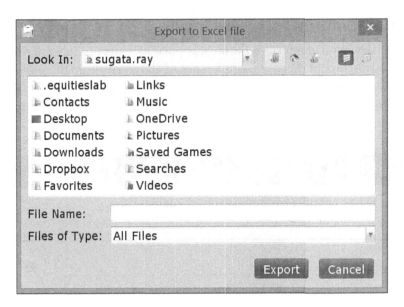

Figure 7.4 Creating the exported file

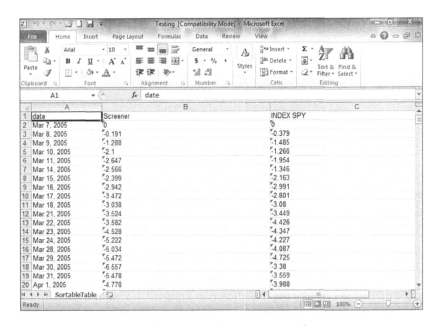

Figure 7.5 Initial export into Excel

Note that all cells are formatted as text, rather than numbers. To convert the data to numbers, first select the data. A small pop-up box with an exclamation point (like the one shown in Figure 7.6) will appear to the left of the selected data. Click it, and one of the options in the drop-down menu should be Convert to Number. Click that, and your data will be converted to numbers.

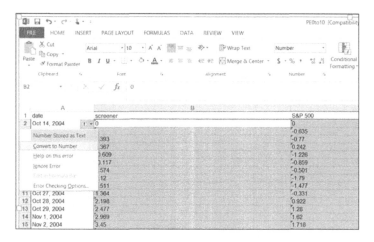

Figure 7.6 Converting export to numbers

Once everything is converted to a number, you can generate a daily series of returns. Add 100 to each number (=100 + screener return) in the Screener column and then generate returns using this formula: return = value today / value yesterday – 1. See Figure 7.7.

	A	B	C	D
1	date	screener	What 100 would becom	Daily return
2	Oct 14, 2004	0	100.00	
3	Oct 15, 2004	0	100.00	=C3/C2-1
4	Oct 18, 2004	0.393	100.39	
5	Oct 19, 2004	0.367	100.37	
6	Oct 20, 2004	-0.609	99.39	
7	Oct 21, 2004	-0.117	99.88	
8	Oct 22, 2004	0.574	100.57	
9	Oct 25, 2004	0.12	100.12	

Figure 7.7 Computing daily returns

Once you have a return series, you can compute average daily returns and standard deviation of daily returns using the =average() and =stdev() commands (see Figure 7.8).

	A	B	C	D
1	date	screener	What 100 would becom	Daily return
2	Oct 14, 2004	0	100.00	
3	Oct 15, 2004	0	100.00	0.00%
4	Oct 18, 2004	0.393	100.39	0.39%
5	Oct 19, 2004	0.367	100.37	-0.03%
6	Oct 20, 2004	-0.609	99.39	-0.97%
7	Oct 21, 2004	-0.117	99.88	0.50%
8	Oct 22, 2004	0.574	100.57	0.69%
9	Oct 25, 2004	0.12	100.12	-0.45%
10	Oct 26, 2004	0.511	100.51	0.39%
11	Oct 27, 2004	1.364	101.36	0.85%
12	Oct 28, 2004	2.198	102.20	0.82%
13	Oct 29, 2004	2.477	102.48	0.27%
14	Nov 1, 2004	2.969	102.97	0.48%
15	Nov 2, 2004	3.45	103.45	0.47%
16	Nov 3, 2004	4.512	104.51	1.03%
17	Nov 4, 2004	4.587	104.59	0.07%
18	Nov 5, 2004	5.906	105.91	1.26%
19	Nov 8, 2004	6.105	106.11	0.19%
20	Nov 9, 2004	6.567	106.57	0.44%
21	Nov 10, 2004	7.432	107.43	0.81%
22	Nov 11, 2004	8.095	108.10	0.62%
23				
24			Average	=average(D3:D22)
25			Standard deviation	=stdev(D3:D22)

Figure 7.8 Computing average and standard deviation of daily returns

Converting average daily returns to weekly, monthly, or annual ones would require multiplying by 5 (weekly), 21 (21 trading days in a month), or 250 (about 250 trading days in a year).[5] Converting daily return standard deviations to weekly, monthly, or annual return standard deviations would require multiplying the daily return standard deviation with the square root of the number of days in the new interval. So, for example, to compute annualized return standard deviations from daily return standard deviations, you would multiply the daily return standard deviation by 15.8 (which is the square root of 250).

Alphas

Alphas are a way to compute the absolute return of a trading strategy. Because it's well known that the market outperforms risk-free investments (such as CDs) on average, holding stocks that are more sensitive to the market will increase exposure to this reward.[6] However, that increased exposure also comes with increased risk. This sensitivity to the market is called *market beta*. It is computed by estimating the sensitivity of a stock's returns to the market's return, after subtracting the risk-free rate from both.

Because risk-free rates at the daily or monthly level are pretty small, relative to stock and market movements, a good approximation could be to regress the stock's return (on the y-axis) against market returns (x-axis) and use the slope from that regression as a measure of the sensitivity.[7]

The intercept on such regressions is known as the *alpha* and represents the risk-adjusted outperformance of a stock or strategy.

In Excel, after computing the returns for the screen and the market using the technique described previously, you can compute alpha and beta using the =intercept and =slope commands, respectively (see Video 7.2). Alternatively, you can graph the regression and add a linear trendline and its equation to see the alpha and beta. Finally, if the Regression Package has been installed in Excel, you can also run a regression to obtain the alpha and beta. Figure 7.9 presents a graph of a regression, along with examples of the =intercept and =slope command.

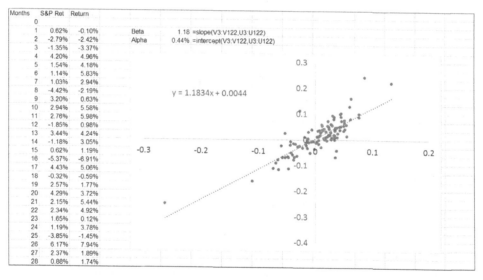

Figure 7.9 Computation of alpha and beta for monthly returns for 0 < PE < 10 screen

The stocks with PE between 0 and 10 screen has a monthly beta of 1.18. This makes it fairly sensitive to the market. If the market were to go up 1%, stocks in this screen would be expected to go up 1.18%. The alpha is 0.44%, monthly. Annualizing this (either the simple way by multiplying by 12, or by compounding) yields an annual outperformance of 5.3% to 5.4%, which is consistent with the outperformance of this screen versus the market (see Figure 7.10).

Figure 7.10 Ten-year backtest of 0 to 10 PE strategy

The screener returns about 275%, whereas the market returns about 100%. That means $100 in the screener would become $375, whereas $100 in the market would become $200 over the ten years. The alpha of the screener is 5.4% per year, so over ten years, the screener would outperform the market by $(1 + 0.054)^{10}$, or 1.85 times $(200 \times 1.85 \approx \$375$, or roughly what is returned by the screen). This only works because the beta of the screen is very close to one. Otherwise, you would have to adjust the market performance by the beta factor.

This means that alpha can be thought of as an annualized outperformance, after taking into account how sensitive a screen's returns are to the market. There are also other, more sophisticated ways to compute alphas, after accounting for the sensitivity of returns of a strategy to not just market returns, but also returns to other known outperforming strategies. Mathematically, the equation for modeling returns using such a regression would be as follows:

$$r_{strat} - r_{rf} = \alpha + \beta_1(r_{mkt} - r_{rf}) + \beta_2 r_{factor2} + \beta_3 r_{factor3} + \ldots + \varepsilon$$

r_{strat} is the return to the strategy in a given period. r_{rf} is the risk-free rate that period. β_1 is the beta on market returns minus the risk-free rate $(r_{mkt} - r_{rf})$ in that period. β_2 and β_3 are the sensitivities to other "risk factors." The most common factors used in practice are based on the factors identified in "The Cross-Section of Expected Stock Returns" (Fama & French, 1992). These are the returns to a portfolio of small stocks minus big stocks (also called the "small-minus-big," or SMB, portfolio) and the returns to a portfolio of high book-to-market companies minus the returns to low-book-to-market companies (or the "high-minus-low," or HML, portfolio). These are available on Ken French's Web site at http://mba.tuck.dartmouth.edu/pages/faculty/ken.french/data_library.html.

You can download these series and regress the returns on your strategy on the factors you want. The intercept from the regression is the alpha of the strategy.

Video on alpha computation: http://bookvid72.sugata.in

Other Measures of Interest

There are other performance measures that may be of interest to investors using a quantitative strategy. You can compute these in Excel relatively easily. Rather than walk through the calculation, the following list enumerates some of these and gives the intuition behind them:

- **Maximum drawdown**—Maximum drawdown is the maximum consecutive loss in a trading strategy. As an example, look at the backtest for a strategy in Figure 7.11 (it doesn't matter what the strategy is). The maximum drawdown occurred from the peak in late 2007 to the trough in early 2009. $100 invested in the strategy would have grown to $150 at the peak, and fallen to about $30 at the trough. Thus the maximum drawdown would be about a (1 – 30/150) or an 80% loss.

Figure 7.11 Example to compute maximum drawdown

- **Best/worst months**—This is self-explanatory. A lot of investors used the best and worst months (and second, third, and so on best and worst months) as a measure of volatility. In fact, there is a class of risk management tools that focuses exclusively on the worst *x*% of months/weeks/days. These measures are known as value at risk, or conditional value at risk measures and are briefly described later in this list.

- **Value at risk (VaR)**—This is one of the standard risk measures out there. Value at risk expresses how much money (or how many percent returns) you would lose in a worst-case scenario. The worst case is quantified by a percentage level and a time horizon. So, for example, the sentence, "Our 1% value at risk at the daily level is $100,000," would mean that in the worst 1% of days, the investor would lose at least $100,000. There are three key aspects to this sentence: The first is the 1% level, the second is the word *daily,* and the third is the amount that is at risk. Basically, all value at risk statements have these three components. You can compute hypothetical value at risk numbers from backtest results by looking at the worst days or months for a given strategy.

- **Conditional value at risk (CVaR)**—CVaR is very similar to VaR, except that rather than reporting the minimal loss in the worst-case scenario, CVaR reports the average loss in the worst-case scenario. "Our 1% conditional value at risk at the daily level is $100,000" would mean that in the worst 1% of days, the investor would lose, on average, $100,000. CVaR at a given level is generally higher than VaR at the same level.

- **Dividends paid**—This is a measure of the average dividend yield of a strategy. Some investors care deeply about a steady source of cash flow (retirees, for example) and will be very interested in this measure.

- **Turnover**—This is a measure of how frequently the holdings in the investor's portfolio are traded (or turned over). It is typically expressed as a percentage of assets under management transacted annually. For example, if you manage a $1 million fund and trade a total of $2.5 million worth of stocks during a year, your average annual turnover is 250%. The higher this number is, the higher transaction costs are likely to be.

- **Sharpe ratio**—Sharpe ratio is a measure of return, controlling for risk. It is typically computed by dividing the average annualized returns above the risk-free rate by annualized standard deviation of returns. So, for example, the S&P 500 has outperformed the risk-free rate by about 6% over the last 50 years and its standard deviation of annual returns is about 15%. This leads to a Sharpe ratio of about 40%. Note that Sharpe ratios across different horizons are not directly comparable. The monthly Sharpe ratio is likely to be a lot lower than the yearly

Sharpe ratio. This is because returns scale close linearly, whereas standard deviation scales by the square root of the increase in period. So, using the numbers from the previous example, the average monthly return for the S&P 500 would be about 0.5% and the monthly return standard deviation would be 3.5%. The monthly Sharpe ratio would thus be about 14%.

- **Appraisalratio**—Appraisal ratio is very similar to the Sharpe ratio, except the numerator is the alpha of a strategy and the denominator is the standard deviation of residuals from the alpha regression. That is, for each year, compute the "expected" return of the strategy as alpha + beta × market return that year. The difference between this and the actual return for the strategy is it basically adjusts the returns for standard risk factors before calculating the ratio. As before, the ratio is not comparable across different time horizons for the reasons mentioned previously.

The Results Summary Tab

Many of these performance measures are available in the backtest summary tab. Figure 7.12 shows a screen of companies that lose money within our usual Restrictions tab.

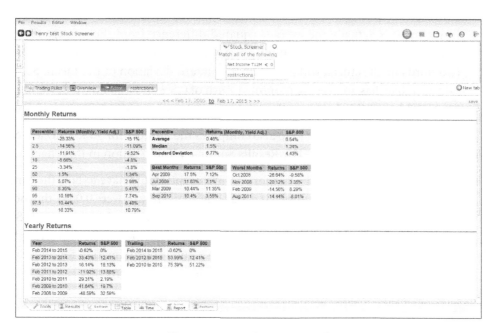

Figure 7.12 Results summary tab

You can see that many of the measures discussed are in this tab, for example, the average returns, the standard deviation of returns, and some of the best and worst months. All of these are compared against the comparable statistics for the S&P 500. As expected, money-losing companies don't do well compared with the market as a whole.

As mentioned earlier, Equities Lab is an evolving piece of software. Thus, the data in the results summary tab will change occasionally to continue to incorporate results that users find of interest. If there's a particular field you are interested in having in the results summary tab, e-mail support@equitieslab.com and put in a request. If enough people ask, it will be put in.

Endnotes

1. Raw returns are simply returns. Practitioners and academics often qualify returns with the word *raw* to emphasize that no adjustments have been made to the return numbers and they would accurately reflect an investment's growth.

2. One of the dirty tricks of the mutual fund industry is some conniving fund managers retroactively choose and change their benchmark indices such that their historical fund performance beats the index. This practice has been documented in a study by Berk Sensoy (Sensoy, 2009).

3. In reality, it is actually the average squared difference from the average return, square rooted. In terms of intuition, an easy way to think of standard deviation is two thirds of all returns will lie within a standard deviation of the mean. So, if I said a strategy has an average monthly return of 0.5% and a standard deviation of 5%, roughly two thirds of months will have a return between -4.5% and +5.5%.

4. The backtest result summary tab also computes the number for you. You can read more about this tab in the "The Results Summary Tab" section in this chapter.

5. This is an approximation. To be more accurate, you would have to take the exponent, rather than simply multiply. If the average daily return were 0.05%, the more accurate average weekly return would be $(1 + 0.05\%)^5 - 1 = 0.250250125\%$, rather than simply 0.25% (0.05% × 5). This effect of compounding gets larger for longer periods, so the simple multiplication is a good approximation for obtaining weekly or monthly returns, but not as good for annual returns.

6. The average annual outperformance of the market versus the risk-free rate (T-bill rate) has historically been about 6%. It is called the *market risk premium.* This is the reward investors in the market get for the risk they bear. Any academic textbook will discuss this in great depth in the chapter on the Capital Asset Pricing Model (CAPM).

7. Finance textbooks will have a slightly different, more accurate computation of beta and alpha, using the CAPM. Specifically, they will subtract the risk-free rate from both market returns and from the stock returns. However, because risk-free rates don't change that much on a day-to-day basis, simply using raw returns gives a fairly good approximation of beta. The alpha computed is also fairly accurate, but has slightly more error for high beta stocks. You can obtain data on the risk-free rate if you want to do the more accurate analysis from the U.S. Treasury Web site at http://www.treasury.gov/resource-center/data-chart-center/Pages/index.aspx.

8

Rebalancing—Why, How, and How Often

Rebalancing is the process by which the stocks in a screen are closed out at the end of your strategy's horizon and the proceeds are reinvested into the stocks in the screener for the following period. The basic tension in deciding how often to rebalance is that the more frequently you rebalance, the more you trade—and the higher your costs are. The benefit of more frequent rebalancing is that your positions are based on fresh information.

Costs of Rebalancing More Frequently

Costs of rebalancing are most often either financial costs (for example, paying your brokerage firm a commission to trade stocks) or labor costs (for example, logging in and executing all the transactions needed to rebalance your portfolio).

Financial Costs

The biggest difference between backtest results and actual money made would likely arise from financial costs associated with transactions.[1] These transaction costs stem from four main sources: (1) commissions paid on trades, (2) the bid ask spread, (3) moving the market, and (4) taxes.

Commissions

Commissions are the most straightforward type of transaction cost. Each trade made on your brokerage will result in a brokerage commission cost. This can range from $1 per trade (on Interactive Brokers) or less (Motif Investing charges $9.95 to trade entire baskets) to hundreds of dollars per trade on some of the traditional Wall Street brokerage houses. These commissions would erode into your realized returns because they would be paid out of your capital base. For example, if you started investing with $100,000, and bought 50 stocks, paying $10 per trade, you would lose $500 right off the bat (or an immediate negative return of –0.5%).

Although there is no easy way to integrate these costs into the Equities Lab structure, it is easy to estimate the magnitude of their effect using some data from the backtest graphs. Consider the two strategies shown in Figures 8.1 and 8.2. Both use the same strategy (investing in the top ten value stocks, ranked by how they did in the last year).

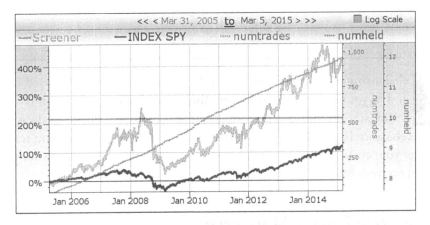

Figure 8.1 Value and momentum—monthly rebalance

Figure 8.2 Value and momentum—quarterly rebalance

The monthly rebalance strategy rebalances three times as frequently as the quarterly rebalance strategy. However, its performance is also better. You can estimate the commission-based transaction costs using the *numtrades* series. Do this by creating a new tab, called plot_numtrades; the only field in the tab will be Number of Trades.

Similarly, you can plot the number of holdings by creating a tab called plot_numheld with the content being Number of Held Positions. In the monthly rebalancing system, by the end of the ten years, the strategy has made about 1,000 trades, whereas in the quarterly rebalancing system, the strategy only makes about 500 trades. At $10 cost per trade, the transaction costs are cumulatively $5,000 (500 trades × $10 per trade) lower for the quarterly rebalance than for the monthly rebalance. You can weight that against the outperformance to see if it's worthwhile doing a monthly rebalance.

> **TIP**
>
> The *Number of Trades* variable plotted in *numtrades* tracks the number of holdings that have changed. For equal weighting, you must also make small adjustments to positions that don't change over a rebalance. In practice, traders often just don't adjust those positions and let the weights deviate a bit from equal. If you included trading the unchanged positions, the number of trades would simply be 1,200 (10 holdings × 10 years × 12 rebalances a year) for monthly rebalances and 400 for quarterly rebalances. Some newer brokerages (such as Motif Investing) also allow trading of entire baskets of stocks, so transaction costs would only be assessed per rebalance, regardless of the number of positions traded. In this case, computing the cost would involve comparing 120 monthly rebalances to 40 quarterly rebalances.

Transaction Costs—Spreads and Price Impact

In addition to explicit transaction costs, you also incur the bid ask spread. The bid ask spread is the difference in price between which you can buy a stock and sell a stock. An example will make this clear. Take a look at Microsoft (MSFT), as shown in Table 8.1.

Table 8.1 Information on Microsoft—Excerpted from Yahoo! Finance

Microsoft Corporation (MSFT)		(Information excerpted from Yahoo! Finance.)	
47.51	up 0.61 (1.30%)	2.49 PM - EST Nasdaq Real Time Price	
Prev. close	46.90	Day's range	46.68–47.74
Open	47.00	52wk range	34.93–50.05
Bid	47.44 x 4500	Volume	19,956,751
Ask	47.45 x 1600	Avg. volume (3m)	34,733,100
1yr target est.	49.57	Market cap	391.62B
Beta	0.69	PE (ttm)	18.62
Earnings date	26-Jan	EPS (ttm)	2.55
		Div & yield	1.24 (2.60%)

Microsoft last traded at $47.51. However, the market has fallen since that last trade. The current best bid (the highest price someone is willing to buy at) is $47.44. The best offer (the lowest price someone is willing to sell at) is $47.45. The bid ask spread in this case is one penny. If you bought and sold Microsoft immediately at posted prices, you would lose one penny for each share that you transacted. Of course, even if you bought now and sold three months later, if the price had not moved and the bids and asks were exactly the same, you would still lose that same penny. This is the contribution of bid ask spreads to transaction costs.

In the case of Microsoft, the bid ask spread is not terribly material (one penny divided by a $47.51 stock is a 0.02% loss from the bid ask spread). In the case of a less liquid stock, the bid ask spread would be more significant. For example, Table 8.2 shows the Yahoo! Finance screenshot for Natural Resource Partners (NRP).

Table 8.2   Natural Resource Partners LP Information—Excerpted from Yahoo! Finance

Natural Resource Partners LP (NRP)		(Information excerpted from Yahoo! Finance.)	
9.52	up 0.06 (0.63%)	2.58 PM - EST Nasdaq Real Time Price	
Prev. close	9.46	Day's range	9.30–9.92
Open	9.46	52wk range	9.30–20.72
Bid	9.49 x 200	Volume	1,289,521
Ask	9.51 x 300	Avg. volume (3m)	755906
1yr target est.	14.83	Market cap	1.16B
Beta	1.46	PE (ttm)	7.28
Earnings date	Feb 11-16	EPS (ttm)	1.31
		Div & yield	1.40 (14%)

Here, the bid ask spread is two cents on a $9.51 stock. The bid ask spread would result in a loss of 0.21% when trading this stock (two cents divided by $9.52).

However, the bid ask spread is only one component of this cost. The prices may also move against you as you try to trade. The *x 200* and *x 300* following the best bid and best ask indicate the depth of these offers. What x 200 means is that up to 200 shares can be sold at $9.49. After you sell those 200 shares, the next best bid will be lower than $9.49. If you are trading larger positions, you will end up moving the market during your trades. This is an added transaction cost, known as price impact.[2] Again, note that for very liquid stocks like Microsoft, this is unlikely to be a major factor in transaction costs. Looking back at Table 8.1, the bid and ask depths for MSFT are x 4500 and x 1600, an order of magnitude more than NRP.

Transaction Costs—Taxes[3]

The final transaction cost is tax. Positions that are sold at a gain incur capital gains tax. Depending on how long you have held the position, that might be a short-term capital gains tax or a long-term capital gains tax. Against this, you can deduct losses in positions that you have closed on which you have lost money.

In general, if you rebalance at any reasonable frequency, taxes will cut into positive returns generated by successful quantitative strategies. Let's demonstrate with a concrete example.

Using a value and momentum screen, with a quarterly rebalance (Figure 8.2 has the backtest for this strategy), I will estimate the amount of taxes assessed. I'll assume a 20% tax rate on any gains each year, along with a refund of 20% of any losses.[4] Figure 8.3 shows how $100 invested in this strategy would have done without taxes and with taxes.

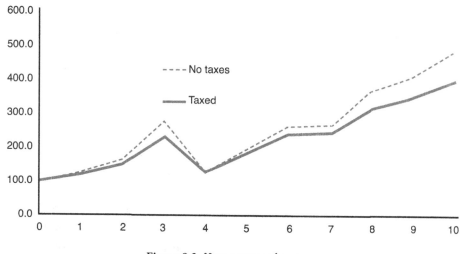

Figure 8.3 How taxes erode returns

We can see that the cumulative effect of taxes over the ten years ends up being about $80 (for a $100 investment).

Of course, the good news is that you must be making gains to have taxes, so these are psychologically easier transaction costs to bear because you are only paying them when you are profiting. The other piece of good news is that a number of account types (such as Roth IRAs) are tax exempt and do not require you to pay these taxes.

"In this world nothing can be said to be certain, except death and taxes."
—Benjamin Franklin

Labor Costs

Labor costs have two components. The first is a fixed component to beginning any quantitative strategy. For example, you must read this book, you must open a brokerage account after deciding which one is best, you must run some strategies in Equities Lab to figure out which one is best for you, and you must monitor your positions in between rebalance periods. The second type of labor cost is variable in how often you trade. These are probably almost directly proportional with trading commissions. Every time you rebalance your portfolio, you must log in to your brokerage account and implement a set of trades. Some of these costs can be mitigated by choosing the right broker, but they will still exist.

You can't do much about the fixed labor costs. In fact, given that you're already midway through this book, you might not feel fixed labor costs of doing quantitative research are actually *costs* but are actually educational experiences that are closer to being *benefits*. For the variable labor costs, you can minimize these in the same way you minimize commissions—rebalancing less frequently or holding fewer securities in your portfolio.

Minimizing Labor and Transaction Costs

As mentioned, the easiest way to minimize costs is to minimize the number of transactions. You can do this by rebalancing less frequently. The tension in choosing a rebalancing period is between these transaction costs and the benefits of basing your positions on fresh information. Of course, the most frequently you *can* rebalance is the frequency with which your information is released. If you are trading on any information that relies on prices, that means you can rebalance every instant (because that is how frequently prices change). However, if you are investing based on accounting disclosures (such as the Piotroski F-score), you probably should not rebalance more frequently than every month.[5]

Just because you can rebalance every time your information changes does not mean you have to. Unless information changes a lot, rebalancing will often end up being a time-consuming process that produces few changes in the portfolio.

It will take a bit of judgment to determine if your screening strategy is based on information susceptible to massive changes in a given period. I can provide two examples. Let's say you have a screener based on accounting profitability (picks stocks with the top

1% return on assets [ROA]) and another screener based on returns over the last three months (picks stocks with the top 1% returns in the last three months).

Moving from a monthly to quarterly rebalance will affect the latter much more than the former. For starters, in the former, only those companies that have filed a new quarterly statement in the last quarter will likely be affected. Even then, it is unlikely that total assets (the denominator in ROA) will have changed much. Income might change a bit, but is much more persistent than stock returns. On the other hand, the momentum strategy of picking companies with the top 1% of returns may change considerably in a month.

Testing this empirically, the cumulative changes in the portfolio over ten years of back-tests are as shown in Table 8.3.

Table 8.3   Effect of More Frequent Rebalancing on Number of Transactions

	Top 1% ROA	Top 1% Quarterly Return
Monthly rebalance	863	1,148
Quarterly rebalance	627	584

In the quarterly rebalance, both trade about 600 times over ten years. However, moving to the monthly rebalance, the momentum strategy almost doubles the number of trades, while the ROA strategy only increases trades by 50%.

To summarize the point, in this case, shifting to a monthly rebalance will be less painful for the ROA strategy than for the momentum strategy.

The gain from switching rebalancing periods can also be empirically computed from backtests. However, in general, winning strategies tend to perform better when they are rebalanced more often (before transaction costs). Comparing the added returns with the transaction costs will provide some measure of whether the increased rebalance is worthwhile.

As an example, let's return to the monthly versus quarterly rebalance of the value and momentum strategy documented in Figures 8.1 and 8.2. Suppose you're trading a portfolio of $200,000, and your brokerage charges $10 per transaction. The 100% over ten years would mean you'd be making $200,000 more over the period. However, the added transaction costs would consume at least $5,000 of that.[6] In this case, the quarterly rebalance would likely be worth doing. If, on the other hand, you had $20,000 to trade with, the benefit of the quarterly rebalance would be less clear because the additional 100%

would only yield $20,000, of which a significant fraction would be consumed by transaction costs.

Optimal Rebalance Frequency

As you can see from the previous example, a variety of factors can affect how often you should rebalance your quantitative trading strategy. The most obvious of these are:

- Portfolio size
- Projected gain from more frequent rebalancing
- Number of holdings in portfolio and additional trades from more frequent rebalancing
- Transactions costs
  - Explicit commissions
  - Bid ask spreads (depends on stock liquidity)
  - Price impact (depends on stock liquidity)
  - Taxes
  - Labor costs involved in rebalancing more frequently

Remember that another way to reduce transaction costs in quantitative strategies is to reduce the number of holdings in your quantitative strategy. For example, rather than saying, "I want all the stocks that pass my screening criteria to be held equally," you can hold up to five or ten stocks that pass your screen, ranked by some criteria (as we did in the previous example). This might mean that if you are using a screen that allows many stocks to pass through, you might end up with a lower rebalancing period; however, if you cap the holdings of the screen, you might be able to rebalance more frequently because the transaction costs of rebalancing are lower.

I have empirically experimented with these numbers and settled on a quarterly rebalance as being optimal for a wide range of trading strategies and portfolio sizes. The reason that the quarterly rebalance is optimal for a wide variety of strategies is that many trading strategies use accounting data, which is updated quarterly. Thus, more frequent rebalancing often results in fewer (and less meaningful) changes in the portfolio. Less frequent rebalances miss out on significant changes in accounting numbers. If you are not interested in doing your own analysis to determine an optimal rebalance frequency for your strategies, consider the quarterly rebalance as a default strategy.

Endnotes

1. Of course, past performance is never an indication of future performance, so the biggest difference is probably going to arise from the future not exactly mirroring the past.

2. In this case, a sale of 200 times $9.49 or $1,898 would be sufficient to lead to a drop in price. Any added shares beyond the 200 would execute at a price lower than $9.49.

3. The tax section is for information only and does not constitute tax advice. Tax laws change frequently. Consult a tax professional for tax advice.

4. This assumes that capital losses can be deducted against income or against capital gains in other accounts.

5. Although it is true that accounting information is released quarterly, the fact that companies have staggered release dates means that information for some companies in your portfolio will likely change during any given month.

6. This $5,000 number is computed simply by eyeballing the number of trades in the quarterly rebalance (500) and the number of trades in the monthly rebalance (1,000), taking the difference, and multiplying it by the $10 per trade. In reality, there would also be other transaction costs, such as the headache of a monthly rebalance and additional taxes.

9

Weights—Equal or Otherwise

W eighting refers to the allocation of capital among stocks that initially pass through a screen. This book has mainly dealt with equal weighting. This means the capital is equally divided among all the names that pass through the screen. This is one of the most common weighting systems in practice because of its simplicity and because of its performance characteristics. Equities Lab currently only supports equal weighting during rebalances, so the following discussion on weighting is unfortunately not accompanied by empirical analysis from Equities Lab. However, this chapter does discuss several other weighting schemes and the rationale for using them. The ability to support custom weighting schemes is on the list of planned features for Equities Lab and should be added to Equities Lab in the near future.

Market Capitalization Weights

Using market capitalization weights basically assigns portfolio components weights according to the ratio of their market caps. So if a portfolio had two companies and their market caps were $50 million and $150 million, the portfolio would be one quarter invested in the first company and three quarters invested in the second one.

This is by far the most common weighting scheme in the world. Many indices weight constituents by market capitalization. For example, the S&P 500 index weights the 500 components by their respective market components.[1] The beauty of market cap weights is that there is no need to rebalance. At the end of the year, because all assets would have grown in proportion to the growth in their market caps, the weights will automatically reflect each asset's current market cap. You would have to execute trades to rebalance the portfolio only if you were changing the constituents of a strategy.

This automatic, frictionless rebalancing when using market cap weights has several advantages. You save on commissions. You also minimize taxes generated by trading out of winning positions. However, market cap weighting also has disadvantages. In particular, in backtests, market cap weighting strategies generally underperform their equal weight (or almost any other weighting scheme) counterparts.[2]

Empirically, equal weighting has had a fairly good run compared with market cap weighting, and there are a number of equal-weighted index funds that have emerged recently. In particular, the Guggenheim S&P 500 Equal Weight ETF (ticker RSP) has gained some traction and has handily outperformed the SPY (market cap weight S&P 500 ETF) over the past decade (see Figure 9.1).[3]

Figure 9.1 SPY (market cap weights) versus RSP (equal weights)

Of course, if you start with the premise that equal weighting is better than market weights, than weighting by the inverse of the market caps should be even better! And empirically, it is. However, this runs into potentially larger transaction costs because you would be buying more of the smaller cap names within the portfolio, which are also likely to be less liquid and have higher transaction costs.

Fundamental-Based Weights

Fundamental weights refer to the practice of weighting companies in a portfolio by some fundamental characteristics. Two common characteristics, both popularized by WisdomTree funds, are dividends and earnings.

Dividend weighting assigns weights to companies according to the magnitude of dividends a company paid in the past year. WisdomTree's dividend weighted index (on which a number of its funds are based), is constructed as follows:

> The WisdomTree Dividend Index is a fundamentally-weighted index that defines the dividend-paying portion of the U.S. stock market. The Index measures the performance of US companies, listed on the NYSE, AMEX or NASDAQ Global Market, that pay regular cash dividends and that meet other liquidity and capitalization requirements established by WisdomTree. The index is dividend weighted at the annual reconstitution in December to reflect the proportionate share of the aggregate cash dividends each component company is projected to pay in the coming year, based on the most recently declared dividend per share. The index was established with a base value of 300 as May 31, 2006.
>
> —From the WisdomTree Web site

According to analysis from the WisdomTree Web site, this weighting scheme has also outperformed the market cap weighted Russell Index. In both the case of dividend weight and the case of earnings weighting, only companies with a positive value for the weighting criteria are included (that is, only dividend payers are included in the dividend-weighted index and only positive earnings companies are included in the earnings-weighted index).

Ultimately, if you decide on a nonequal weighting scheme, be sure to have a sense of what changing the weighting scheme is likely to do to your returns. If, for example, you move to dividend weights, you should expect your strategy to generate a higher yield than equal-weighted backtests would suggest. Similarly, if you move to market cap weights, performance may lower but that may be offset by lower transaction costs. When the weighting feature is activated in Equities Lab, you will be able to empirically backtest whatever weighting scheme you are interested in to determine how the strategy would have performed in backtests using different weighting schemes.

Endnotes

1. The Dow Jones Industrial Average and the Nikkei 225 use a wacky weight: raw price level! They literally use the price of the stock to weight it. A $100 dollar stock has ten times the weight of a $10 stock in these indices.

2. This is potentially because there is a natural "buy-low, sell-high" feature baked into equal-weighted strategies that is not there in market cap weighted strategies. In an equal-weighted strategy, at the end of your rebalance period, you will trim positions on which you have made gains (and the price has gone up), while increasing positions where you have lost (and the price has gone down). Thus, there is a natural "buy-low, sell-high" feature built in to this weighting scheme. In the market cap weighting system, this is absent.

3. Additionally, one of my former students did a similar study for the German DAX companies and found a similar pattern for those stocks.

10

Some Powerful Screens

T here is an entire industry dedicated to developing quantitative screens that make money. In fact, there are multiple industries dedicated to this. There is, of course, an industry of money managers who create and follow quantitative techniques. There is also an academic industry that looks for anomalous stock returns. Quantitative screens that generate significantly positive returns are anomalies because if market prices truly reflected all publicly available information about a stock, it should not be possible to generate high returns by screening based on this publicly available information. Academics are not content with simply documenting an anomaly and quietly profiting off of it. They will also proceed to find creative explanations for why these anomalies exist and why they should persist despite efficient markets. You'll read more about this academic view in Chapter 16, "Why Does Quantitative Investing Work?"

This chapter draws on the wisdom of others who have preceded us in the field of quantitative investing and shows how to replicate their screens yourself. In the process, you will also develop a sense of how the screens have performed recently and which stocks are passing through these screens currently. Each of the first three sections in this chapter is dedicated to a single, historically successful screen developed by someone much smarter (and probably much richer) than me. I will document the publicly available information about the screen, and using this data, I will attempt to create the screen in Equities Lab and evaluate recent returns. The chapter concludes with a discussion of two screens that are "new." One is a screen I created and another is a screen created by Henry Crutcher, the founder of Equities Lab. Of course, they are not truly novel, in the sense that people have developed similar screens before, but rather, they are distinctive and produce sufficiently strong backtests that it is worth mentioning them separately.

Piotroski F-Score

This is probably one of the hottest screens out there today. It is based off an influential paper written in 2000, "Value Investing: The Use of Historical Financial Statement Information to Separate Winners from Losers" (Piotroski, 2000). The F-score is based off of nine criteria. Companies earn one point for each of the criteria that they satisfy. The final score ranges from zero (the worst) to nine (the best). The nine criteria are divided as follows:

- Four profitability criteria

  - Return on assets (ROA)[1] > 0

  - Cash flow from operations (CFO)[2] > 0

  - ROA in the past year > ROA two years ago (or ROA is increasing)

  - CFO > net income (this assigns a point if the company actually makes more money than accounting income because accounting income can be fudged more easily than CFO)

- Three financing/financial health criteria

  - Leverage fell over the past year (where leverage is $\frac{\text{Long-Term Debt}}{\text{Total Assets}}$)

  - Liquidity increased over the past year (where liquidity is simply the current ratio, or $\frac{\text{Total Current Assets}}{\text{Total Current Liabilities}}$)

  - If the firm did not have any equity issuances in the past year

- Two operating efficiency criteria

  - Margins (defined as $\frac{\text{Revenue} - \text{Cost of Goods Sold}}{\text{Revenues}}$) increased over the past year

  - Turnover ($\frac{\text{Revenues}}{\text{Total Assets}}$) increased over the past year

Recall that for each criterion that a company meets, the company earns a point. This leads to the F-score, a number that ranges from zero to nine: the higher, the better.

In the paper, Piotroski finds that companies with an F-score of nine outperform companies with an F-score of zero by 23% per year over the period from 1976 to 1996. Even after accounting for other factors (such as value, as measured by book to market), high F-score firms still significantly outperform low F-score firms.

The good news about the F-score is that it is pretty easily re-created in Equities Lab (see Figure 10.1). The even better news is it has already been created for you!

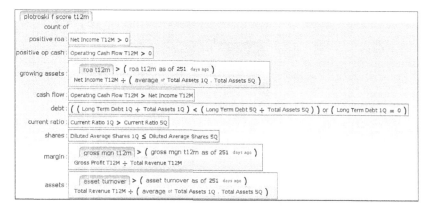

Figure 10.1 Equities Lab re-creation of Piotroski F-score

To use this precreated formula in a screen, simply create a new screener, and press Ctrl+Shift+F to pull up a list of formulas. Choose either the yearly or trailing 12-month version of the Piotroski F-score and choose the slices you want.

Comparing the outperformance of eight and nine F-score stocks (top line in Figure 10.2) to those of zero or one F-score stocks (bottom line in Figure 10.2), you see the significant annual outperformance. Additionally, high F-scores outperform the S&P, whereas low F-scores lag the S&P.

Reassured that the screen works even in the recent ten years (which are not in the original period examined by Piotroski), you can safely put the F-score screen to work and either buy the stocks with high F-scores, or short the stocks with low F-scores, or both.

Another way to use the F-score is by adding it to any other screen you generate to enhance your returns. For example, you can add a Piotroski screener to a value screener to make sure that the companies that are cheap relative to earnings also have healthy earnings and financing situations. The strategy and backtest are presented in Figure 10.3.

The results are dramatic. The 0 to 10 PE screen combined with the Piotroski F-score of more than seven returns six times over the last ten years. This is higher than either of the two screens separately.

Figure 10.2 F-score > 7 versus F-score < 3

Figure 10.3 Adding an F-score criteria to a value screen

The Magic Formula

This is the famous formula of legendary investor Joel Greenblatt. He writes about it in his book, *The Little Book That Beats the Market* (2005). This is a value investing book that combines two separate metrics of value, earnings yield and return on capital, and generates a list based on these metrics.

Earnings yield is computed as $\dfrac{\text{EBIT}}{\text{Enterprise Value}}$. Earnings Before Interest and Taxes (EBIT) is a common proxy for the cash flows of a company. Enterprise value is the value of all parts of the capital structure, or financing components, of the firm. This typically includes the market value of all shares traded, as well as the value of the debt of the firm. Cash is typically subtracted from this sum as it can technically be returned to investors, reducing amounts owed to them.

Return on capital (ROC) is a similar ratio; however, instead of dividing EBIT by enterprise value, ROC divides it by a book measure of capital:

Net Fixed Assets + Current Assets – Current Liabilities

Once these two measures are computed, the Magic Formula ranks all stocks in the universe by these measures, and then sums the two ranks. So, for example, if Company A is ranked 20 based on earnings yield, and ranked 30 based on ROC, the total rank score is 20 + 30, or 50. Once the combined ranks are generated, the Magic Formula then advocates investing in a fixed number (between 30 and 50) of companies with the lowest combined ranks.

To generate this list in Equities Lab, you first need to create formulas for earnings yield and return on capital and then generate a combined rank of earnings yield and ROC (Figures 10.4 and 10.5).

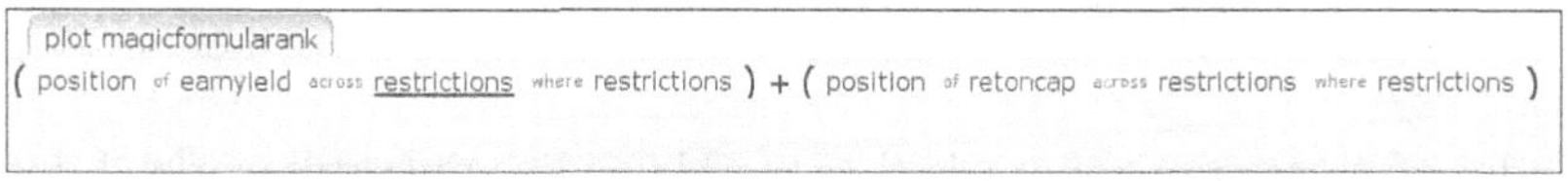

```
plot magicformularank
( position of earnyield across restrictions where restrictions ) + ( position of retoncap across restrictions where restrictions )
```

Figure 10.4 Combining ranks of earnings yield and ROC

Earnyield and Retoncap are computed as shown in Figure 10.5.

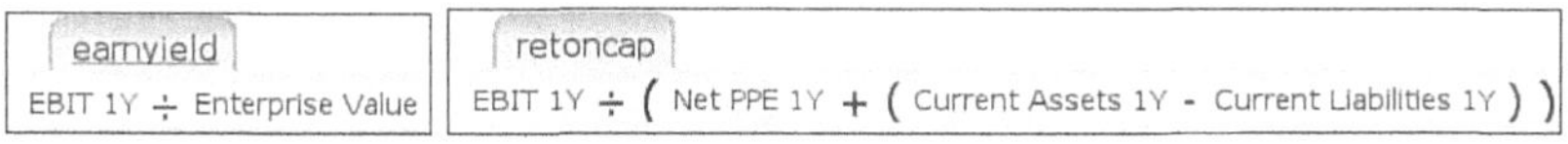

```
earnyield
EBIT 1Y ÷ Enterprise Value
```
```
retoncap
EBIT 1Y ÷ ( Net PPE 1Y + ( Current Assets 1Y - Current Liabilities 1Y ) )
```

Figure 10.5 Computing earnings yield and return on capital in Equities Lab

Finally, the Restrictions tab is similar to the one from before. The only thing the editor does is screen for restrictions. However, the Trading Rules limit the number of positions to 25 (or however many stocks you want to hold), ordered by the combined Magic Formula rank multiplied by −1, as shown in Figure 10.6.[3]

Figure 10.6 The screening and ordering criteria in the Magic Formula screen

The long-run historical backtests (see Figure 10.7) have been great, as per Greenblatt's book. The screen made money over the last ten years. Also, because Greenblatt kindly discloses the stocks returned by the Magic Formula, it is possible to match up the stocks returned by Equities Lab with those returned as per www.magicformulainvesting.com/. I detected an overlap of up to half the names, but I could not recover the entire list.

Figure 10.7 Backtest performance of Magic Formula

There is a lot of discussion about whether the Magic Formula still works. I don't know whether it still works. My naïve guess from the backtest results in Figure 10.7 would lead me to the conclusion, "Probably, to some extent." That being said, I might be wrong. There are a wide variety of Web sites and blogs that pop up when you Google the phrase, "Does Magic Formula investing still work?" Other Web sites and the revised edition of the Magic Formula book give different (sometimes more favorable, sometimes less favorable) backtest results than mine. However, the advantage of Equities Lab results is that I actually know where they come from. I can re-create each day of trading. If the return for a month or a day looks off, I can double-check all the returns for all the stocks in the portfolio on that day. Backtest results from opaque sources (such as from Web sites or even those from the book itself) don't give me the same level of comfort.

The Value-Momentum Combo

This is another combination screen, similar to the screener discussed in Chapter 3, "Creating a Screen—The Nuts and Bolts of Choosing a Quantitative Investing Strategy," in the section "A Real-Life Screener." In this case, the screen combines value and momentum concepts (see the "Value Screener" and "Momentum Screener" sections in Chapter 3). The concept was detailed in an academic paper, "Value and Momentum Everywhere" (Asness, Moskowitz, & Pedersen, 2013), where the authors document the presence of these two strategies working in a wide variety of markets, and even more important, working together to create a screener that is more powerful than either screener individually.

How to Combine Multiple Criteria in a Single Screen

Before explaining the screener itself, let's discuss exactly how to combine two or more criteria. There are two ways to combine the screens. The first is simply investing in all stocks that pass either screen. So, because you know that value stocks outperform and high momentum stocks outperform, you would buy both value stocks and winners. This is represented graphically in Figure 10.8, and logically, coding this on a computer would involve picking stocks that pass either the value screen OR the momentum screen (or both).

Another way to combine two screens would be to require stocks pass both the screens before you invest in them. Graphically, these are presented in Figure 10.9. If you just picked the intersection of the lowest PE and highest momentum stocks, you would be left with the dark square in the upper left. Sometimes, this does not leave enough stocks to form a well-diversified portfolio, so you might need to loosen the screening criteria for both metrics, in which case, you would include the gray shaded area, making up a larger square.

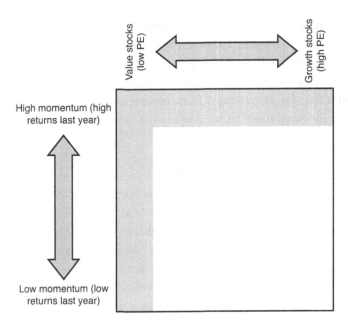

Figure 10.8 Combining two screens by picking stocks that pass either screen

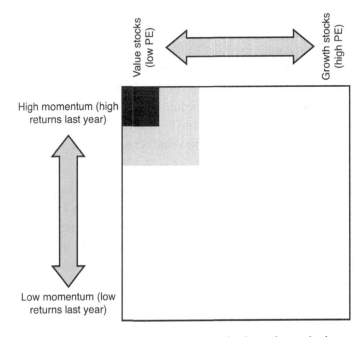

Figure 10.9 Combining screens by picking stocks that only pass both screens

These are the two main ways to combine screens. I prefer the latter (requiring stocks to pass both screens). The former (picking stocks that pass either screen) is basically the same as investing half your money into value and half into momentum. It's actually slightly worse because the stocks in the intersection (both value and momentum stocks) are only picked once. Of course, picking the intersection runs into problems if too few stocks are in the intersection. If that is the case, you can relax the individual criteria for each metric.

My implementation of a value and momentum intersection screen looks like Figure 10.10.

Figure 10.10 Backtest of value and momentum

I pick stocks that are in the top 20% of earnings yield (this is a measure of value) for a given sector *and* have returns in the last year that are in the top 20% for the sector. I do this after running the standard set of exclusions in the Restrictions tab. Running the backtest with a quarterly rebalance, this strategy yields a nice return of about 250% over the last ten years. Additionally, the number of holdings is between 3 and 35, making it a fairly tractable strategy to re-create.

This outperformance was documented in "Value and Momentum Everywhere" (Asness, Moskowitz, & Pedersen, 2013) over the last 30–40 years, and across a number of markets. In the paper, the authors mention that this outperformance is susceptible to crashes, and consistent with this point, we also see a significant dip in the strategy backtests during the 2008 crisis. However, the good news about the strategy is that after the crisis, it recovered well and continues to outperform the markets.

A Defensive Screen

In addition to a few of the screens created by others, I'm also including a screen that I like a lot. It has elements from screens discussed previously, but it also has some unique elements. I call it a defensive screen, in the sense that it is designed to go down less than the market when the market goes down. Of course, this also generally means that the strategy is also less sensitive on the upside. Regardless, fine-tuning the parameters has led to a performance and risk profile I find attractive in backtests.

The key things I'm looking for here are stable, big companies, with low betas and good earning power. The "big" part ensures that these companies are not going to completely crater during a financial crisis. The "low beta" part ensures that when the market goes down, these companies do not go down as much.

Coding this into Equities Lab, we have the usual Restrictions tab (with market cap cutoff raised to $5 billion). In the screener, I focus on companies with low betas and high earnings yield, picking the intersection of the ten lowest beta and ten highest earnings yield stocks in each sector, as shown in Figure 10.11.

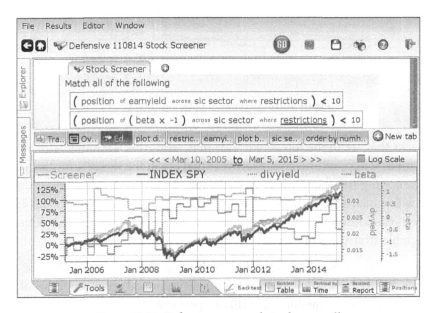

Figure 10.11 Defensive screen, relative beta cutoff

The portfolio performs acceptably over the last ten years, especially given the large size and low betas of the companies in it. The returns are higher than the S&P 500, and the standard deviation is lower. An interesting thing to note is that during the financial crisis of 2008, the portfolio fell as much (or more) than the markets. This was a particularly confounding observation during the crisis that all assets had very high correlations, regardless of how sensitive (or insensitive) they were supposed to be. The other interesting thing is, despite picking the lowest beta stocks, the beta of the portfolio has crept up to the point where it is close to 1 (0.9 to be precise). This tends to happen sometimes, where choosing a relative cutoff for your screens can lead to a drift in the factor you are trying to control for. Another way to control for this would be to simply put an absolute beta cutoff (see Figure 10.12).

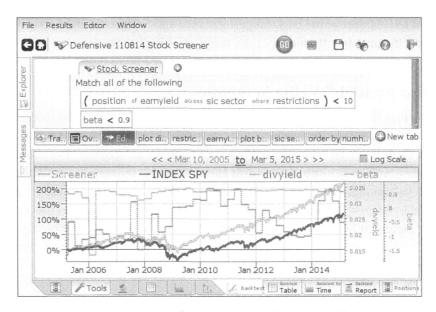

Figure 10.12 Defensive screen, absolute beta cutoff

This turns out to be a better backtest, but because the beta cutoff is hard-coded in, the number of holdings tends to be lower (generally in the mid 20s, rather than the full 30; at only 19 stocks today). The returns are even higher than before, and the standard deviation is even lower. After running these two screens, you can make an informed decision regarding which you like better. I personally like the second screen more.

It is tempting to pick parameters solely on the basis of backtest results when comparing two techniques to execute a screen (for example, relative versus absolute beta cutoff for the defensive screen). However, you should also consider other factors, such as the average number of holdings in the screen and potential differences in risk measures, before choosing the final screen parameters.

As you can see, both of these defensive screens have some value flavor, favoring high earnings yield.[4] The innovations here are the low beta and the big size, which is what makes the screens pick "defensive" stocks. Many screens you create yourself will have this theme, where you pick some known factors (for example, value) and add a couple of layers to it to (1) improve the backtest performance and (2) fine-tune the screen to meet a more specific investment objective than simply making money.

A "Good Enough" Value Screener

This is the first screen in which I am going to demonstrate the potentially huge backtest results that Equities Lab can generate, given the right strategy. This is a strategy created by Henry Crutcher, which he calls the "good enough" value screener. It uses the power of satisficing to significantly outperform the market, by looking for stocks that pass "enough" valuation metrics, each of which looks for good "enough" value on a metric. In particular, the first pass of the screen looks for stocks that pass seven of the ten criteria shown in Figure 10.13.

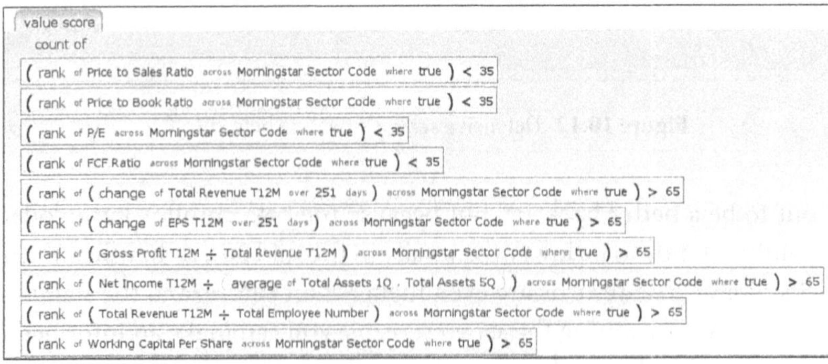

Figure 10.13 Value criteria for "good enough" value

This screen doesn't select a stock because it is a superstar in one valuation metric; it has to be good on a collection. The screener then takes the surviving stocks and takes the ten with the best improvement in various growth metrics, as shown in Figure 10.14.

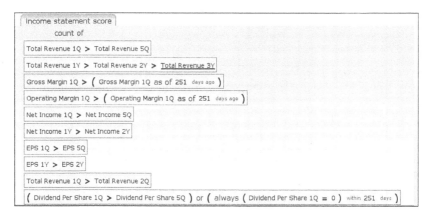

Figure 10.14 Income statement score for "good enough" value screener

Again, this screen doesn't look for companies that overwhelm one attribute; any sign of improvement across several metrics is given more weight. In essence, the companies that are cheap enough are ranked by how much of their income statement is good enough.

The backtests show a 10x return over the past decade (see Figure 10.15). Whenever you see backtests of this magnitude, it is a good idea to dig further to see if there are one or two outliers driving the results. The performance is analyzed by year, market capitalization, and industry in Figure 10.16.

Figure 10.15 Backtest of "good enough" value score

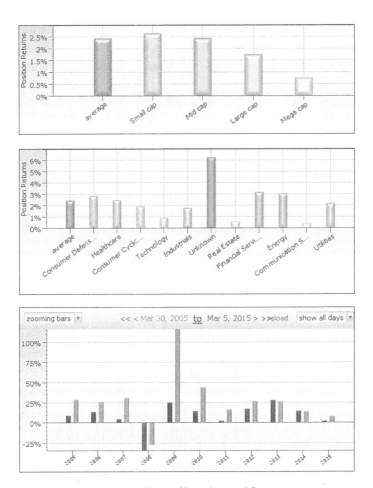

Figure 10.16 Slices of "good enough" screener

Returns in 2009 look really good, and small caps outperformed slightly. Finally, the previous backtest rebalanced weekly, which isn't terribly realistic (although it is doable for a ten-stock portfolio, especially when the payoff is a 10x decade). Let's go all out to stack the deck against us: standard restrictions from "The Restrictions Tab" section in Chapter 3, quarterly rebalancing, and skipping over 2009, as shown in Figure 10.17.

Even with the deck completely stacked against it, it has a 3x decade. This seems investable. We've tweaked parameters, eliminated good years, tested for extreme concentration, and tried different rebalance frequencies. The "good enough" value screener survives these tests and exposes the power of strategies that you can develop using the principles of quantitative investing.

Figure 10.17 A handicapped implementation of the "good enough" value screener

Endnotes

1. ROA is defined as $\dfrac{\text{Net Income}}{\text{Total Assets}}$.

2. CFO is computed by taking net income and adjusting it for noncash revenues and expenses. For example, you would add depreciation (a noncash expense) back in.

3. Because Equities Lab orders from largest to smallest, when picking the 30 stocks out of all that pass the restrictions, you need to multiply the Magic Formula rank by −1 so that lower ranks are picked to filled the 30 slots.

4. Earnings yield, or EBIT divided by enterprise value, is very closely linked to PE. Inversing the PE ratio give earnings to price, which would be almost equivalent to earnings yield for a firm with no debt (scaled to a constant for the tax rate). Earnings yield simply includes debt in the denominator, while adding back interest in the numerator and is a more holistic measure of the income generation power for the firm as a whole, without considering leverage.

11

Where to Get Ideas for New Screens

After seeing the screens in this book, you might be wondering how to generate ideas for screens yourself. A tempting, but ultimately flawed way of generating screens is to just keep experimenting with variables and cutoffs, running backtests, and then picking a backtest that performs well. The perils of this approach were covered in Chapter 3, "Creating a Screen—The Nuts and Bolts of Choosing a Quantitative Investing Strategy," in the "Aimless Screens" and "The Problem with Building Strategies Solely to Outperform in Backtests" sections.

Similarly, Chapter 3 also covered the importance of linking screened variables to economic fundamentals that you are interested in. For example, if you are interested in generating an income stream out of a fixed capital base, you should be screening for dividend yield.

However, that still does not give you a whole lot of guidance on how to generate new ideas. Ultimately, this is where the "secret sauce" lies. Sophisticated investors who use quantitative techniques are fiercely proprietary about their sources of outperformance. Put differently: If you found a variable that had perfect predictive power over future returns, would you be in a rush to share it with the rest of the world?

Despite the proprietary nature of quantitative ideas, there is one steady source of ideas that I consult: academic research. There is a rich and growing literature in finding variables that predict future stock returns and explaining why they predict future stock returns. These variables that predict future stock returns are known as either anomalies or risk factors. In academic papers, something observable today that predicts future returns is known as an *anomaly*. If that something is correlated with a source of priced risk as well, such as market betas, it becomes a *risk factor*. So, for example, market beta is a risk factor because we know that high beta stocks *should* provide higher returns than low beta stocks in exchange for a higher correlation with market returns. However, there is little consensus on whether, for example, the F-score is an anomaly or a risk factor.

Until an academic researcher documents firmly that the F-score is tied to some measure of risk that should be priced, the F-score remains an anomaly, in the sense that picking high F-score stocks beats the market. Chapter 16, "Why Does Quantitative Investing Work?" discusses these concepts further.

In either case, a quick review of academic finance articles with the words "anomaly" or "risk factor" should provide fertile ground for ideas for screens.

Understanding an Academic Article in Financial Journals

Once you've found an article you think is interesting, you will need to skim through it to decide if it can be helpful to your screening process. I'll start by picking a famous paper I've used before in discussing my value screens, "The Cross-Section of Expected Stock Returns" (Fama & French, 1992). In this article, the authors propose that in addition to sensitivity to market returns, the value orientation and size of the stock also affect future returns. I have discussed value at length, so I will focus on the size effect, as documented in the paper. Table 11.1 is an excerpt from Table II of that paper.

Table 11.1 Excerpt from Table II on Size Effect from Fama and French (1992)

Size Bin	Smallest 5%	5%–10%	10%–20%	20%–30%	30%–40%	40%–50%	50%–60%	60%–70%	70%–80%	80%–90%	90%–95%	Largest 5%
Return	1.64	1.16	1.29	1.24	1.25	1.29	1.17	1.07	1.10	0.95	0.88	0.90
Representative size ($ million market cap)	7.24	24.05	37.71	60.34	90.02	132.95	200.34	307.97	512.86	915.99	1619.71	4628.55

This table, and many similar tables in academic studies, sorts stocks into bins, based on some variable. In this case, it is size (or "ranked valued of ME [market equity] for all NYSE [New York Stock Exchange] stocks on CRSP [Center for Research in Stock Prices]," according to the original paper). You can see that as the size bins increase, the market capitalization increases from 7 million to many billions. More interestingly, and of more direct use to us, is the fact that future returns (based on size today) decrease along this sort, from a high of 1.64% monthly returns as the average return for smaller stocks, to a low of 0.90% for the larger stocks.

You don't really need to know anything else from this table. Smaller stocks outperform. Now you can take that knowledge and test it out with your own data. Until 2007, before the crash, the performance was almost perfectly inversely related to the size slice, as shown in Figure 11.1.

Figure 11.1 Performance by size slices until 2007

After the crash, however, the performance across the size slices is not that different, as shown in Figure 11.2.

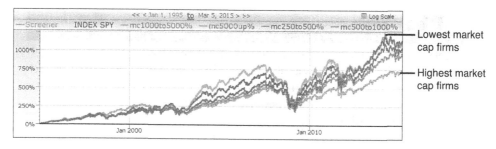

Figure 11.2 Performance by market cap slices (including period after 2007)

As you can see, the size premium does not look like it still exists. Indeed, over the last two decades, a number of studies have cropped up challenging the existence of the size premium, including the article, "Three Analyses of the Firm Size Premium" (Horowitz, Loughran, & Savin, 2000). The abstract states, "In our analysis, we use annual compounded returns, monthly cross-sectional regressions, and linear spline regressions to investigate the relation between expected returns and firm size during 1980–1996. *All three methodologies report no consistent relationship between size and realized returns.* Hence, our results show that the widespread use of size in asset pricing is unwarranted" (italic emphasis is mine). The paper proceeds to show that the size effect during this period was clustered only in the month of January, and the remainder of the months showed no visible size effect (see Figures 1 and 2 in the original paper). Graphs are another way academic papers will present results, and these are very similar to tabular sorts.

A third way that academic papers present findings is using regression techniques. A regression is basically fitting a line through the points on a chart. The idea is that some variable (size) explains another variable (future returns). The regression technique generally imposes a linear relationship between the two, and the slope of the relationship is presented, along with a measure of statistical significance. Returning to the original paper, "The Cross-Section of Expected Stock Returns" (Fama & French, 1992), the regression results are presented in Table III of the paper.

Each row in Table III of the paper presents regression, and the second row shows the regression of future returns on size. The slope is negative, coming in at −0.15. The number below the slope, −2.58, is called the t-statistic, or t-stat. It conveys how statistically significant the relationship is. T-stats of above 2 are considered statically significant. For negative slopes, t-stats are generally presented as a negative number, so in these cases, t-stats of below −2 are considered significant.[1]

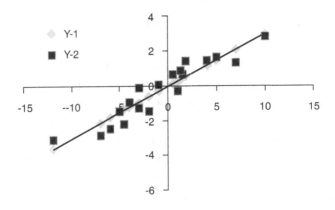

The slope of −0.15 means for each unit increase in ln(ME), or the natural log of the market capitalization in millions, the expected monthly future return decreases by 0.15%. Again, the main thing you need to note is the directionality (size is *negatively* linked to future returns), and you can do your own tests.

Where to Find Academic Finance Articles

Now that you know how to understand salient features of an academic finance article, you might be wondering where to find these articles. One source is a set of finance journals that are published periodically. Skimming the bibliography of this book will give you the names of a few of these journals. Unfortunately, academic finance, like many other academic disciplines, has reached a state where there is a backlog of articles waiting to be published in these journals. Thus, papers that are in the most recent journal issues tend to have been written years ago. For the most recent cutting-edge research, you can check papers that are being presented in the major conferences. (The American Finance Association, the Western Finance Association, the European Finance Association, and the Financial Management Association meetings are the four large finance conferences.) Alternatively, you can check out the Social Sciences Research Network (SSRN). The SSRN is a prepublication site where authors can post versions of their working papers as they progress through the academic publication process. Note that because anyone can post anything on SSRN, and there is no peer review before posting, you should use results in SSRN papers cautiously, and always double-check their validity against your own empirical work.

Other Sources of Ideas

Some of you will also have ideas of your own. For example, you notice that every time *X* happens, the markets go up. An example might be the weather. You live in New York and notice that every time there's bad weather, the markets tend to go down.[2] One way to check this might be to obtain a record of weather in New York and then see if stocks do go up on days with good weather and down on days with bad weather. Then if you find this is indeed the case, you could trade based on the weather forecast.

In general, wherever data is easily available (weather, accounting numbers, sports scores, demographics, and so on), other quantitative investors have looked at the data. When data is less easily available, there may be scope to find a "new" predictive factor. Despite the difficulty in finding a "new" quantitative idea, there's little reason not to exploit existing known factors that are continue to predict future returns.

Endnotes

1. The relationship between β and future returns, for example, is not statistically significant.

2. In case you were thinking of actually testing this, don't! Someone's already done it. The paper, "Stock Prices and Wall Street Weather," looks at exactly this effect and finds that on days with heavy cloud cover, stocks perform poorly compared with days with little cloud cover (Saunders, 1993).

12

Troubleshooting

Troubleshooting, or fixing errors, is important in the context of building quantitative strategies. Generally, the only way you would know that something is wrong is by examining the results of either the backtests or the screens. This section deals with the troubleshooting process:

- Identifying "wrong" results

- Locating potential coding errors leading to "wrong" screens or backtests

- Reconciling backtest results with your prior beliefs regarding a strategy when the two are not consistent with one another

Apart from troubleshooting in the process of building strategies, troubleshooting during implementation is also important. This chapter does not address concerns regarding implementation, but Chapter 14, "How Do You Actually Make Money Now? A Brief Guide to Implementation," does have a short discussion on this in the section, "Will My Strategy Make Me as Much Money as My Backtests Suggest?"

What Are "Wrong" Backtest Results/Screen Results?

Sometimes, you think that a strategy should work well, but after doing some backtesting, you realize it does not work well. Or perhaps you think a screen should be returning about 100 stocks, but after looking at the results, you see it is returning only a handful. These are situations in which you have potentially "wrong" results.

In general, before running a screen, you should have some sense of three to four stocks that should pass through. For example, if you are running a large cap, growth stock screen, you would expect companies such as Netflix, Google, and the like to pass through. The first sign that something is amiss would be if these companies do not pass through the screen.

Similarly, when you run backtests, you should have a rough sense of what the results should look like. For example, if you are screening for value stocks (for example, $0 < PE < 10$), you might expect that the strategy should outperform the overall market. You might suspect this because you read about the outperformance of value stocks in Fama and French (1992). When you run your backtest, you find that the strategy does not outperform. This is another example of "wrong" results.

Of course, not all screens and backtests lend themselves to easy diagnosis like these examples. However, after running 20 to 30 different screens, you should have some idea of what does what. Specifically, when you run a new screen after trying 20 or 30 different ones, you will know generally what other screens this new screen relates to, and you will have a sense both of the names that should pass through the screen today, as well as how the screen should perform in backtests.

Coding Errors

Suppose you find a situation in which either the holdings being screened are not quite right, or the backtests are not quite right. There could be two possible reasons for these seeming errors: (1) There's something you're not coding correctly, leading your results to defy your expectations, or (2) your initial belief motivating your strategy is wrong. This section can help you determine if you have an error in your quantitative trading strategy.

There are two ways to troubleshoot quantitative strategies. The first is reconstructing the strategy you are aiming for, one criterion at a time. The idea is that when you add the incorrect criterion, you'll see an immediate response in the results that will alert you: "This criterion is the one wreaking havoc with the results!"

This technique can also be used in reverse. That is, you can remove criteria from a misbehaving screen until it starts producing results that are more consistent with expectations. Here, the key to troubleshooting any strategy is to remove conditions one by one, until you arrive at results that make more sense. Then focus on the criterion that you have removed to see if its removal fixed the problem.

Once you know the troublesome criterion, you can decide whether to leave it in or keep it out after examining what stocks it screens out and why.

Your Prior Belief Is Wrong

So, if after looking for coding errors and finding none, you still have results that seem wrong, you are left with the only alternative explanation: Your initial belief about the strategy is wrong. You can draw this conclusion based on the results of empirical analysis, which often produces results inconsistent with the initial hypothesis. As a scientist, I have been frustrated when the data does not prove what I had believed was true. However, I am also flexible enough to accept that my initial hypothesis was wrong in these cases.

If an initial backtest yields questionable results, further empirical analysis may help convince you that your initial beliefs might not have been entirely accurate. For example, you had a strong belief that fast-growing tech companies are a good sector to invest in. You run the following screen (shown in Figure 12.1) and find the screen (large cap tech, sales growth more than 30% over the last year) to be selecting companies that you like (Facebook and LinkedIn). However, to your horror, you also find such a strategy would have performed horribly over the last ten years. You check your code and find no mistake. You also run several other permutations (perhaps using earnings growth and different market capitalization cut-offs) and find that the lackluster performance is robust to these permutations.

It turns out these fast-growing tech darlings turn out to be no better than the market! Even worse, they are much riskier than the market. This analysis leaves you with no option but to change your mind. Of course, this is easier said than done because you acquired your belief through years of reading about these companies in the media and seeing astronomical returns to companies that matched the screen. However, the power of having the data and tools to easily perform the analysis yourself is that you can eventually convince yourself that your original viewpoint was perhaps incorrect.

In general, the data-driven nature of quantitative investing allows us to distance ourselves from many of the subjective biases that might otherwise drive our decisions. This is discussed in the following chapter on behavioral biases.

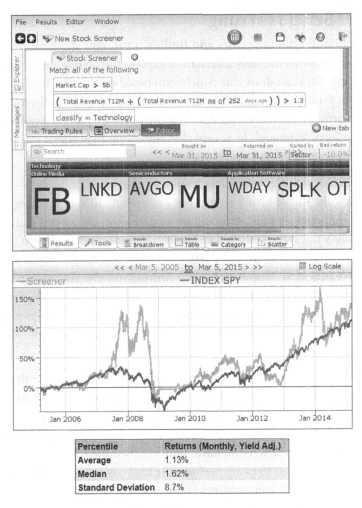

Figure 12.1 Backtest of fast-growing tech companies

13

Behavioral Biases Avoided by Investing Quantitatively

One of the main reasons retail investors do not perform as well when directly trading stocks compared with index mutual funds is that their trading decisions suffer from behavioral biases. Behavioral biases are consistent biases that affect human decisions, impeding our ability to make wealth-maximizing decisions. This chapter enumerates some of these biases and discusses how they affect traditional, but not quantitative investing, and how quantitative investing avoids the negative effects of these biases.

The first three biases this chapter examines have to do with the way many people pick stocks. People read about something in the news, and that in turn leads to some research, which might then lead to a trade. For example, suppose you see a favorable news article about Tesla and the good work they are doing building high-end electric cars. You start with a favorable impression of the company, and you start researching the company and its financial prospects. After a while, without reaching any definitive conclusions, you stop doing research. A few days later, you see another positive article on Tesla, vaguely recall that your fundamental research had yielded positive results and then you make a trade, buying the stocks.

This process has at least three biases in play, as discussed in the following sections.

Recency Bias

The first bias in this process is the recency bias. People's brains are hardwired to over-weight information they have learned recently. If you read a lot about Tesla in the news, you will think about Tesla when it comes time to invest. This bias tends to favor growth stocks. Growth companies do *new* things, and as such, are likely to make it into the *news*.

Of course, from all you have learned about quantitative investing and research in this book, you know that growth stocks are likely to perform worse than value stocks.

Unfortunately, very few news outlets cover steady, nonexciting businesses that have a steady cash flow stream. Thus, the recency bias tends to lead people away from value stocks and toward growth stocks.

Confirmation Bias

The second bias the Tesla example exhibited is a confirmation bias. Once you read the positive news article about Tesla, and you are predisposed to a long position, your subsequent research is going to be tainted by the confirmation bias. Specifically, the confirmation bias leads you to subtly direct your research to *confirm* your hypothesis. You might choose search terms such as "Tesla patents" to research what patents Tesla holds. Of course, you should also be searching for patents held by Tesla's competitors.

Park, Konana, Gui, Kumar, and Raghunathan study this bias (and the overconfidence bias discussed later in this chapter) in their paper, "Confirmation Bias, Overconfidence, and Investment Performance: Evidence from Stock Message Boards" (2010). They study stock market message forums in South Korea and find evidence of confirmation bias where investors tend to favor forum messages that are aligned with their own views. These are also investors who trade more often, tend to be more overconfident (as measured by their self-rated investment prowess), and, ironically, have poorer realized performance.

Source Amnesia Bias

Finally, this section discusses the third bias in the example: source amnesia. This is not a bias per se, but the observation that people tend to forget where they have seen or heard about a piece of information. In this case, you read a positive news article about Tesla and did some nonconclusive research immediately following your reading of the positive article. When you revisit Tesla analysis a few days later, you might confuse the fact that the research was inconclusive and the article you read was positive and just remember that you did research and developed a vague positive impression.

In professional fund management, procedures are adopted to minimize the effects of these biases. Fundamental research analysts keep copious notes on their research process, so they remember exactly what they have done. Also, when a fund manager is interested in a stock, and asks his or her analyst to research it further, the manager will generally not reveal if he or she is interested in buying or selling the stock. This ensures that the analyst is not subject to confirmation bias. Individual retail investors can also keep detailed notes to avoid source amnesia. However, the subtle pressures of the recency and confirmation biases are harder to avoid.

Quantitative trading strategies help people avoid all of these biases by simply removing the scope for the bias to manifest. If you're prone to the recency bias, quantitative techniques will ensure you're picking stocks you've never heard of before. Essentially, by picking stocks based on an objective screen, you avoid having mass media or any other idiosyncratic input affect your judgment. Similarly, because there is very little subjective judgment in quantitative investing, there's no room for confirmation bias in supporting your allocations.

In addition to the three highlighted biases in the previous simple example, the following sections highlight two other biases.

Overconfidence Bias

Human beings are naturally overconfident. The standard example of this is, if asked whether they are an above-average driver, close to 80% or 90% of people say they are. Obviously, this could not possibly be true, as only half of us should be "above average." Thus, people tend to be overconfident. This carries through to investments: People believe the stocks they are picking are the right ones. Park, Konana, Gui, Kumar, and Raghunathan show this in their empirical study of South Korean investors (2010).

How might this bias affect your investing? Perhaps you will invest in a position without knowing enough about the company. Perhaps you will stay in the position despite empirical analysis contradicting the investment thesis in your head.[1] Whatever its manifestation, overconfidence tends to be more frequent where there is some scope for subjective assessment. If you were to survey perceived skills in more quantifiable pursuits (such as 100-meter sprinting times), it is unlikely that the majority of people would say they are above average. Moving away from more subjective assessments of individual stock-picking ability to a verifiable, "backtestable" assessment of quantitative strategy development reduces the scope for this bias to affect the investment decision making process.

Disposition Effect and Loss Aversion Bias

Finally, this section touches on another pervasive behavioral bias that affects retail investor behavior: the disposition effect. The disposition effect is documented extensively by Terrance Odean (1998) in his paper, "Are Investors Reluctant to Realize Their Losses?" Odean hypothesizes that investors are reluctant to realize losses and are overly predisposed to realizing their gains. I'm sure many of us have wanted to "lock in a gain" on a winning position. Also, I'm sure many of us have found ourselves stuck at a blackjack table, trying to "break even." These are all manifestations of the disposition effect.[2]

What does this behavior lead to? In short, it leads to selling winners too early and holding losers for way too long. The disposition effect also tends to trigger higher tax expenditures (because you realize capital gains, but delay realizing offsetting capital losses).

Quantitative techniques completely eliminate the ability to indulge in such lax decision making. For example, the momentum strategy, as described in the "Momentum Screener" section in Chapter 3, "Creating a Screen—The Nuts and Bolts of Choosing a Quantitative Investing Strategy," is designed explicitly to counteract the disposition effect. Historically, the momentum strategy has outperformed. More generally, quantitative investing strategies guide you to buy and sell according to a prescribed system, which means that you have no discretion about whether to sell a stock at a gain or a loss. Thus, quantitative investing largely avoids underperformance resulting from the disposition effect.

How Quantitative Investing Avoids Some of These Biases

Quantitative investing avoids biases by simply prescribing the exact positions you should take (the screened stocks) and for how long you should hold them (the horizon, or rebalancing period). This takes all the subjectivity out of stock picking. There's no room for the recency bias. Most of the names that pass through your screens will be companies that you've never heard of (unless you are explicitly screening for stocks that have been in the news). Nor is the disposition effect a concern. The computer has no psychological compulsion to sell at a gain and avoid a loss—it simply follows whatever rule you establish.

Although this discipline avoids biases at the individual stock level, unfortunately, these biases may arise at the strategy level. This means that instead of applying to a single stock, behavioral biases apply to the whole strategy. For example, the recency bias may rear its head in the fact that you hear about a quantitative strategy in the news and start following it. Another bias that might arise is the disposition effect, in that you may continue losing strategies in an attempt to "break even" on the strategy and prematurely close winning strategies to "lock in a win."

Thankfully, these tendencies tend to be muted by the nature of quantitative investing. In the context of the previous examples, two points highlight why behavioral biases are less likely to be an issue for quantitative strategies. First, very few news outlets cover quantitative strategies, and if they do, it is likely regarding strategies that are based on empirical data analysis such as backtests. Second, because quantitative strategies have fixed rebalance times, it's much less likely you will be tempted to indulge in the disposition effect at the time of rebalance. If anything, quantitative investors will be forced to automatically take stock and decide whether or not to continue a strategy. The most likely factor determining this will be whether the strategy has done well previously. Thus, the opposite of the disposition effect will prevail, with winning strategies continuing and losing strategies cut.

In general, quantitative trading strategies impose an immense amount of discipline on the investing process and reduce the scope for behavioral biases to affect investments. That being said, because we, as humans, are developing and implementing the trading strategies, there is always some chance some bias will affect some portion of the process. Understanding these biases and monitoring your investing processes will minimize your susceptibility to them.[3] Minimizing your susceptibility to behavioral biases, will, in turn, reduce underperformance on their account.

Endnotes

1. I once thought that Netflix would be severely punished by the markets when it became clear that they were basically free-loading off of Internet infrastructure built by other parties. As of this writing, during peak periods, Netflix accounts for about one third of downstream Internet traffic. This actually results in slower Internet overall in residential neighborhoods where everyone is watching Netflix in the evenings. My thesis was that Internet companies would find a way to charge Netflix for this congestion and Netflix's stock would fall as a result. Of course, knowing that I'm a human being with a tendency toward overconfidence, I have not taken a position in this trade. That's probably for the best as I would have lost a lot of money while waiting for my short to bear out (if at all).

2. The disposition effect is rooted in prospect theory (Kahneman & Tversky, 1979). Prospect theory conjectures that humans gain pleasure from gains and feel pain from losses. Additionally, it predicts a gain is less pleasurable than a similar loss is painful. Finally, it predicts that there is desensitization to both gains and losses; twice the gain (or loss) is not twice as pleasurable (or painful). The link between prospect theory and the disposition effect is studied in detail in the paper "What Drives the Disposition Effect? An Analysis of a Long-Standing Preference-Based Explanation" (Barberis & Xiong, 2009).

3. The five biases covered in this chapter are just a small subset of potential behavioral biases that can potentially impact the trading process. For a complete treatment of behavioral biases in finance, an assortment of books is available on Amazon. A simple search for "behavioral finance investing" pulls up hundreds of titles that expand on the behavioral biases documented in this chapter.

14

How Do You Actually Make Money Now? A Brief Guide to Implementation

Implementation of an investment strategy at this point consists of three broad options:

1. Hiring someone else to do it for you

2. Investing in exchange traded funds (ETFs), index funds, or mutual funds

3. Implementing a quantitative investing program yourself

Considering that you're this far into this book, I'm guessing you are probably not that interested in hiring someone to help you manage your money. Alternatively, maybe you have been hired as a financial advisor, and you want to introduce quantitative investing techniques in your portfolio. Hiring someone else to help you implement a quantitative strategy is *sometimes* the right investing strategy, but for many investors, options #2 and #3 often lead to perfectly acceptable financial outcomes.

Buying index funds and holding them can be a smart way to invest. In fact, investors are often advised, "Buy a cheap index fund." It takes virtually no time at all, is tax efficient, and protects your account from wild swings in value.

Unless you think you can do better than the market, it's a good, safe play. Even if you think you can do better (and with the knowledge in this book and a bit of research, I think you probably can do better than the market), you should start your investing career with a large fraction of your money in index funds or ETFs. In addition, there are a number of ETFs that are geared toward certain types of stocks. For example, there are value ETFs, momentum ETFs, and dividend-focused ETFs. So if you want to be exposed to these elements, without having to pick individual stocks, you can start by investing in these ETFs. You can always sell these ETFs to make way for your direct strategies because they are generally very liquid. You'll learn more about the pros and cons of using these types of ETFs to substitute for a quantitative strategy in the "Quantitative Investing If You Are Limited to ETFs and Mutual Funds" section, found later in this chapter.

The third option, investing directly in stocks yourself, is what most of this chapter is dedicated to: taking the lessons from the strategies developed in other parts of this book and implementing them in your own portfolio. Toward the end of the chapter are two brief discussions on the role of a quantitative investing agenda and the expectations of a quantitative investing strategy.

First Steps to Implementation

Before you are ready to implement your trading strategy, you must have a trading strategy that you like. You may use one of the "off the shelf" strategies from this book or you may create a screen yourself, built to suit your own investing purposes. Whatever the screen is, it will produce a set of names, and potentially a set of weights for allocating your money over the names. This section assumes that the weights are equal, although having a different set of weights will not change the overall implementation process significantly.

The idea behind implementing your quantitative trading strategy is you will take the money you have to invest, and divide it among the names returned by your quantitative trading strategy. So, for example, if you had $50,000 to invest, and your quantitative trading strategy returned 25 names, with equal weights, you would invest $2,000 in each of the names.

The Brokerage Account

Of course, to invest this money in stocks, you need a brokerage account. Before discussing which one is "best," take a look at the following checklist for what makes a good brokerage:[1]

- **Trading interface**—Does the brokerage allow convenient trading of entire lists of stocks? If not, how long does it take to find each stock you're trading, specify the amount to trade, confirm that that's what you want to do, and click the Go button? If you place trades on the phone (I hope not!), how long do those phone calls take, and are they giving you some value?

- **Fees and costs**—If it costs you 1% of the trade amount in commissions to place a trade, that's going to dictate you trade infrequently. Very infrequently. Most quantitative investing strategies do not work if costs are that high. That applies to both the commission and the bid ask spread (see the section "Costs of Rebalancing

More Frequently" in Chapter 8, "Rebalancing—Why, How, and How Often," for more detail). It might cost a little bit to do this, but as a test of both the trading interface and the costs, pick some stock that you might buy, and buy a very small dollar amount of it. Then sell it again. Figure out how much money you have lost (relative to the amount you bought). You might want to adjust the bid ask transaction cost upward if you used a smaller position size than normal, but that will give you an idea how much friction is involved. As the position sizes increase, so does the friction, but it should be manageable as long as you do not rebalance too frequently.

- **Statements and accounting**—If you can't understand the statements from your brokerage account, you need to address this issue. You won't need the statements now—you'll need them when you have to explain what happened, or figure out what the cost basis was on some stock. If the statement is merely confusing, dig a bit deeper and see if you can make sense of it—and like it. If it is incomplete, figure out how to obtain a better statement, or, if a more complete statement is unavailable, consider changing brokerages.

- **Margin rates**—Brokerages let you borrow money to buy stocks, using stock in your account as collateral. This is called margin trading. Typically, brokerages let you buy up to two times the value of the stock that you have money. So, if you deposit $10,000 and have a margin-enabled account, you can buy up to $20,000 in stock. The margin rate is the interest the brokerage charges on this borrowing.[2] If you never plan to buy stocks on margin (my recommendation, unless you really know what you are doing), the interest rates charged for going on margin won't matter. These are calculated annually and decrease as you borrow more. Most people who destroy their brokerage account do so by means of margin. On the upside, I have noticed that margin debt is a whole lot cheaper than credit card debt, so if you have credit cards with balances, going on margin to pay them off probably makes sense.

- **Customer service**—If you can't contact a human when you need one (it will come up, but only occasionally), then that's a problem. If the human can't help you, in general, that's even worse. This can be a problem at extremely large brokerage firms, as they are no longer growing, and they are less customer-focused. They also have more layers of management. In general, try calling customer service well before you truly need it to find out what you can expect.

- **Ease of logging in**—This might seem trivial, but if it is difficult to log in, then you won't. This could be a bug, or a feature, depending on whether you are likely to check your account too often.

- **Checks/ATM cards**—This can be incredibly convenient if you plan to use your brokerage account for daily expenses. Some brokerages refund ATM fees and give you checks for free. Others will not even issue ATM cards and check books. Be sure the brokerage you're using has the appropriate level of liquidity for your transaction needs.

After exploring the brokerages out there, I have decided that two are particularly well suited to quantitative equity investing strategies. In addition, any discount broker will suffice, as long as the commissions are not significant relative to the capital you are investing.[3]

The two that work particularly well are Motif Investing and Interactive Brokers.

Motif Investing

Motif Investing (www.motifinvesting.com) markets itself as a platform where users can create *motifs,* or themed groups of stocks and can invest in motifs that are created by themselves, friends, other users, or Motif employees.

These motifs are generally built around popular trends and industry themes. Motifs such as the World of Sports and Wearable Tech allow investors to invest in these particular niches. So, the World of Sports motif, for example, will have stocks of sports companies, and the Wearable Tech motif will have stocks of companies that have wearable tech products on the market.

Although Motif Investing does not explicitly market itself to quantitative investors, its platform works remarkably well for the purpose of quantitative investing. Two features in particular make it excellent for this purpose: (1) It allows the creation of motifs, each with up to 30 stocks in them. It also allows purchases of entire motifs for $10 ($9.95, to be exact) per transaction. (2) It allows holding of fractional shares (with up to two decimal places of granularity).

What these two things mean, taken together, is that you could start a quantitative investing agenda with a strategy that holds up to 30 stocks at a given time, with as little as $5,000, rebalancing quarterly, all for commissions of only $40 per year (or 0.80% erosion of returns). It also means that you do not need to worry about rounding errors when evenly dividing your cash among the stocks in your basket.

Figure 14.1 shows an example of what this would look like. I invested $5,000 into a strategy that was returning 20 stocks.[4]

NAME	SHARES OWNED	PRICE	CURRENT VALUE	COST	GAIN / LOSS	WEIGHT	ACTION
Accenture PLC (A)	3.06	$85.04 (⬇ 0.70%)	$260.22	$250.22	$10.00 (⬆ 4.0%)	5.0%	Trade
AT&T Inc.	7.75	$33.20 (⬆ 0.73%)	$257.30	$250.25	$7.05 (⬆ 2.8%)	5.0%	Trade
Bed Bath & Beyond Inc.	3.39	$75.38 (⬆ 1.91%)	$255.54	$249.17	$6.37 (⬆ 2.6%)	4.9%	Trade
C.R. Bard Inc.	1.50	$172.68 (⬇ 2.41%)	$259.02	$250.50	$8.52 (⬆ 3.4%)	5.0%	Trade
ConocoPhillips	4.07	$63.52 (⬆ 1.11%)	$258.53	$249.90	$8.63 (⬆ 3.5%)	5.0%	Trade
Constellation Brands Inc. (A)	2.76	$110.67 (⬇ 0.99%)	$305.45	$248.81	$56.64 (⬆ 22.8%)	5.9%	Trade
Eli Lilly & Co.	3.58	$73.00 (⬆ 1.23%)	$261.34	$250.42	$10.92 (⬆ 4.4%)	5.0%	Trade
EQT Corporation	3.22	$74.73 (⬆ 1.37%)	$240.63	$251.39	-$10.76 (⬇ 4.3%)	4.6%	Trade
International Business Machines C...	1.66	$154.32 (⬇ 0.75%)	$256.17	$251.22	$4.95 (⬆ 2.0%)	4.9%	Trade
Kellogg Co.	3.89	$66.04 (⬆ 1.93%)	$256.90	$249.62	$7.28 (⬆ 2.9%)	4.9%	Trade
Kirby Corp.	2.96	$72.65 (⬆ 0.08%)	$215.04	$252.61	-$37.57 (⬇ 14.9%)	4.1%	Trade
Laboratory Corp. of America Holdi...	2.47	$115.53 (⬇ 0.51%)	$285.36	$250.85	$34.51 (⬆ 13.8%)	5.5%	Trade
Mattel Inc	8.20	$27.20 (⬆ 1.12%)	$223.04	$250.35	-$27.31 (⬇ 10.9%)	4.3%	Trade
Northrop Grumman Corp.	1.76	$157.43 (⬇ 0.32%)	$277.08	$250.54	$26.54 (⬆ 10.6%)	5.3%	Trade
Pfizer Inc.	8.07	$31.59 (⬆ 0.75%)	$254.93	$250.17	$4.76 (⬆ 1.9%)	4.9%	Trade
Pinnacle West Capital Corp.	3.84	$70.90 (⬆ 0.76%)	$272.26	$248.95	$23.31 (⬆ 9.4%)	5.2%	Trade
Public Service Enterprise Group	6.17	$43.54 (⬆ 0.73%)	$268.64	$250.50	$18.14 (⬆ 7.2%)	5.2%	Trade
Quanta Services Inc.	9.70	$26.63 (⬆ 0.60%)	$258.31	$249.19	$9.12 (⬆ 3.7%)	5.0%	Trade
Quest Diagnostics Inc.	3.95	$71.82 (⬆ 1.03%)	$283.69	$249.76	$33.93 (⬆ 13.6%)	5.5%	Trade
Tyco International PLC	5.95	$41.10 (⬆ 1.46%)	$244.55	$248.89	-$4.35 (⬇ 1.7%)	4.7%	Trade
TOTALS			$5,194.00	$5,003.31	$190.68 (⬆ 3.8%)	100%	

Figure 14.1 Motif stock position report (from Motif Investing Web site)

Motif Investing equally divided that $5,000 into the 20 holdings (or $250 each). You can see the cost basis is very close to the $250 for each stock. I have been lucky so far, and the motif has done well. The strategy is a defensive screener that picks value mega caps, with low beta, and it has held up well, relative to the markets. Motif Investing also conveniently provides a benchmarking against the market, as shown in Figure 14.2.

PERFORMANCE TO DATE

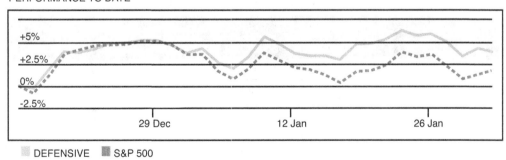

DEFENSIVE   S&P 500

Figure 14.2 Motif performance benchmarking chart (from Motif Investing Web site)

And you can see that the strategy is performing as expected, slowly distancing itself from the S&P 500. This is a strategy that backtests to about 200% in ten years, as opposed to the market, which does about 75%. That difference ends up being about 6% a year, so my outperformance should be about 50 basis points per month.[5] I have been lucky in this month and a half, where my strategy has outperformed by about 2%.

Of course, like any other brokerage, Motif Investing has its drawbacks. The first is that there is a maximum of 30 stocks per motif. If you are interested in a strategy that invests in hundreds of stocks, this will not be a suitable platform. The second drawback is that it currently only allows market orders, which are orders sent for immediate execution. The downside of these orders is that they sacrifice transactional efficiency for immediacy and hence result in paying the full bid ask spread. Returning to the example of Natural Resource Partners (see Table 14.1), a market *buy* order would yield the price of $9.51 (the *ask*). In contrast, many brokerages allow traders to put a *limit* order in. A limit order does not have the advantage of immediate execution, but does allow the specification of a price beyond which the trader will not trade. In this case, I could put a limit order in at $9.50. It will replace the best bid, which is currently $9.49. Now, if there's a seller out there willing to sell at $9.50, they can trade with me.

Ultimately, market orders trade a cheap execution price for guaranteed immediate execution. If your strategies involve large, very liquid stocks (which the Restrictions tab should ensure), market orders will not impose a large penalty. If, on the other hand, your strategies involve trading in illiquid penny stocks, I would strongly advise against using market orders.

Table 14.1   Natural Resource Partners LP Information—Excerpted from Yahoo! Finance

Natural Resource Partners LP (NRP)		(Information excerpted from Yahoo! Finance.)	
9.52	up 0.06 (0.63%)	2.58 PM - EST Nasdaq Real Time Price	
Prev. close	9.46	Day's range	9.30–9.92
Open	9.46	52wk range	9.30–20.72
Bid	9.49 x 200	Volume	1,289,521
Ask	9.51 x 300	Avg. volume (3m)	755906
1yr target est.	14.83	Market cap	1.16B
Beta	1.46	PE (ttm)	7.28
Earnings date	Feb 11-16	EPS (ttm)	1.31
		Div & yield	1.40 (14%)

In summary, Motif Investing is a great platform if your strategies focus on liquid stocks, and have 30 or fewer stocks in them. It is particularly well-suited to investors with a lim-ited capital base because it allows for fractional share ownership.

Interactive Brokers

Interactive Brokers (www.interactivebrokers.com), in many ways, is the perfect comple-ment to Motif Investing. Stocks have to be transacted individually, although the com-mission per trade is a reasonable $1 for orders up to 200 shares. It's very good for trading small, micro, and nano-caps. It's also very good for being able to short stocks that can-not normally be shorted, either because the price is less than $5, or because it is hard to borrow. One of the reasons for these differences is that Interactive Brokers (like most brokerages except Motif Investing) allows limit orders. Of course, placing and managing limit orders is a time-consuming process.

On the downside, the user interface is incredibly complicated (it makes Equities Lab look very simple indeed). Also, they have a minimum monthly fee, which may be waived for larger accounts. The account statements are complete but somewhat confusing at first. Eventually, you will grow used to them. As an aside, you can place trades directly from Equities Lab into an Interactive Brokers account, which saves time. This feature is currently in beta and if you are interested in beta testing this feature, e-mail support@ equitieslab.com and ask for information.

In summary, Interactive Brokers is good for strategies that involve small cap, illiquid stocks. It is also better for strategies that deploy larger amounts of capital because there are no fractional shares available. Finally, it is better for more tech-savvy investors, and it is possible to link tools such as Equities Lab, Java, or Excel to trade directly in Interactive Brokers using an application programming interface (or API). The details on how to do this are available on Interactive Brokers' website or Equities Lab's website.

Discount Brokerages

Aside from these two specific brokerages, there are a slew of discount brokerages out there. These typically have commissions that are low ($4–$20 dollars a trade) and a variety of user interfaces. Common names include Schwab, E-Trade, Ameritrade, Scot-trade, and so on. Many of them (for example, Schwab) have reports you can read about various stocks, and the ability to obtain debit cards, checks, or other conveniences. If you have your money with one of these, and want to start quantitative investing using your existing brokerage, I have nothing to say that would make it worth moving the money to another one.

There are also some among these that have started instituting zero-cost commissions. Robin Hood, a newer mobile trading app, currently in beta, offers free trades.[6] A number of brokerages have free equity trades if you maintain large balances with them (or affiliated entities). For example, Merrill Lynch and Bank of America, at the time of this writing, offer up to 100 trades free per month for customers with $100,000 in combined accounts (this includes any mortgages) with Bank of America.

Even if your discount brokerage offers cheap or free commissions, be sure to check its execution policies. If it is not offering good execution prices (the price you obtain on the trade does not line up well with market bid ask numbers), definitely consider moving brokerages. It is also illegal for market orders to be executed at a price worse than the best quote on the exchanges, so if you ever spot a market order with subpar execution, call your brokerage, and they will fix it.

TIP

"If you don't need to short the unshortable, and/or have larger size trades, then Tradier could be the right brokerage for you. They have a $3.95 commission, for orders of any size. They also have a lot of hookups to software (including Equities Lab), and a clean, simple user interface. I can say from personal experience that their customer service is spectacular."

—Henry Crutcher, founder of Equities Lab

Full-Service Brokerages

Full-service brokers are brokers at big banks. These are the people you call on the telephone to place a trade. Their brokers are typically knowledgeable and helpful. However there are two problems that are, in my opinion, overwhelming:

- **Conflict of interest**—The biggest problem with full-service brokerages is that they are not impartial market infrastructure. They play all sides of the fence, and you may lose out as a result. Perhaps the bank associated with the brokerage needs to underwrite some weird bond offer that will help one of their investment banking clients? No problem—they have all these nice brokerage accounts to sell to. Maybe they have a nice shiny new IPO that needs selling? Again, they have brokerage clients for that! The larger the firm, and the more varied the business, the more interested their "advisors" will be in convincing you to invest in certain products, which will likely not perform well.

- **Fees**—Full-service brokerages have commissions that are incredibly high compared with discount brokerages. Transaction amounts of .5% to 1% of transaction amounts may not be uncommon. Needless to say, with a 1% loss every time you trade, even the best quantitative investing programs will have trouble making money.

The upshot is that, as long as commissions and the conflicts of interest are minimal, any brokerage should be fine. Certain specialized brokerages, such as Motif, are ideally suited for quantitative investing due to their ability to deal in fractional shares and their basket trade capabilities.

Quantitative Investing If You Are Limited to ETFs and Mutual Funds

As you create profitable quantitative investing strategies, you might find yourself asking, "Isn't there an ETF or mutual fund for this style of investing?" This section is designed to help answer this question.

The short answer is, "Yes." There are ETFs and mutual funds for almost everything nowadays. Even if there is no exact fund for your investing strategy, there will likely be one soon.

Let's start with value. If you like value stocks and think their historical outperformance will continue, there is a long list of value ETFs out there. The website www.etfdb.com returns more than a hundred of them, with a few being shown in Table 14.2.

Table 14.2   The First Few Names in a List of Value ETFs from http://etfdb.com/type/style/value/

Symbol	Name	Price	Change	Assets	Avg. Vol.	YTD
IWD	iShares Russell 1000 Value Index Fund	$102.87	−0.42%	$25,214,283	2,047,726	−0.84%
VIG	Vanguard Dividend Appreciation ETF	$80.35	−0.51%	$20,891,506	905,540	−0.36%
VTV	Vanguard Value ETF	$83.29	−0.38%	$17,435,202	1,191,731	−0.82%
DVY	iShares Dow Jones Select Dividend Index Fund	$80.19	−0.80%	$15,702,618	1,135,425	+1.59%
SDY	SPDR S&P Dividend ETF	$78.23	−0.69%	$13,833,306	1,001,745	−0.20%
DIA	SPDR Dow Jones Industrial Average ETF	$176.53	+0.11%	$11,914,502	6,503,953	−0.21%

Symbol	Name	Price	Change	Assets	Avg. Vol.	YTD
VYM	Vanguard High Dividend Yield Index Fund	$68.26	−0.47%	$10,628,643	780,694	−0.07%
IVE	iShares S&P 500 Value Index Fund	$92.24	−0.54%	$8,402,130	783,982	−0.98%
IWS	iShares Russell Midcap Value Index Fund	$74.30	−0.44%	$7,038,266	696,308	+1.25
IWN	iShares Russell 2000 Value Index Fund	$100.06	−0.50%	$6,027,556	1,508,786	−1.13%

Of course, this list highlights the problem you still face. Which of these is the right one? With a strategy created at the stock level, you can tell exactly which stocks to buy out of the value stocks out there. Here, you're faced with more than a hundred value ETFs. You do not know what these ETFs invest in. Despite being billed as "value" ETFs, they may have considerable assets in growth stocks. Additionally, these ETFs are likely to be more expensive than index ETFs.

Rather than spend time trying to figure out if holdings in the ETF match up with holdings in your quantitative strategy, it is often more efficient to simply create a portfolio of stocks directly on your brokerage and buy the stocks directly. A nice bonus is that you save on paying the ETF expense ratios.

That being said, if you truly have minimal assets such that rebalancing (even at the Motif Investing $10/rebalance rate) is not an option, an ETF specializing in the quantitative style you are interested in might be the right answer for you. If you choose to go down this route, you will have to do a bit of due diligence on the ETF or mutual fund you are considering. Specifically, you will have to make sure holdings are broadly aligned with your investment philosophy. Also, you should make sure the fund's expense ratio is low. [7] Remember that these expenses will directly erode your expected outperformance. If you think value investing beats the market by 4% a year (based on backtests), and you invest in a value ETF that charges 0.50% expense ratio, your overall level of outperformance will be reduced to 3.5%.

Will My Strategy Make Me as Much Money as My Backtests Suggest?

After building a strategy and implementing it, you might be hungry for results. Each day, you track how the portfolio is progressing, and you worry if the strategy loses money and are ecstatic if it gains. You track the strategy's outperformance against the S&P 500 (or whatever benchmark you are trying to beat) even more closely.

Stop!

As hard as it is to do this, you should stop looking at your brokerage account every day. Quantitative strategies are designed to be largely "set-it-and-forget-it" type of investments. It might be worthwhile to check in a couple of times during the rebalancing period to see how the strategy is performing, but you only need to check in once the rebalancing period is coming to its end.

This brings me to the subject of this subsection: your performance. If your strategy is sound and continues to work, over the long run, it is likely to be slightly lower than the backtest performance, before transaction costs. Of course, the first part of the sentence, "If your strategy is sound," is a hedge against backtested results of strategies that involve micro-caps, or screens that work only by chance, but are not based on any fundamental drivers of outperformance.

Why should you expect your performance to be slightly lower than backtests suggest? This is because of something called out-of-sample decay. When you construct your strategies, you are picking stocks such that backtest results are maximized (along with many other things, of course). So, if you are screening for value stocks, and you run screens for 0 < PE < 10, 0 < PE < 12, and 0 < PE < 8, and find that the 0 to 10 PE screen does best, you are likely to use that screen as the final screen when you implement your strategy. It is likely that the 0 to 10 screen does best not because it truly is the "best" value screen, but rather, because over the last ten years, stocks just happen to have performed in such a manner to lead the 0 to 10 screen to outperform the 0 to 8 and 0 to 12 screens. This means that the 0 to 10 screen is likely to perform more similarly to the 0 to 8 and 0 to 12 screens going forward. This is known as *out-of-sample decay*. Any time you are devising a screen to outperform, you are subtly influencing it to maximize backtest results. That leads to a little extra boost for backtested returns.

TIP

The name *out-of-sample decay* comes from the fact that quantitative investing relies on relationships estimated with a *sample* of data. Once you try to use the relationship outside the original sample, there is likely to be some decay in the relationship. The easiest way to understand out-of-sample decay is using the following hypothetical situation. Suppose you decide to create a screen based on whether a company's name has and odd or even number of letters. This screen is economically not meaningful and should not affect returns going forward, but let's pretend you do not know that. Backtesting the screen, you find that companies with an odd number of letters (call them *odds*) outperform those with an even number of letters (call them *evens*) by 50% over 10 years, and you correspondingly implement your screen to pick the *odds*.

Out-of-sample decay would suggest that the 50% outperformance would dissipate, or decay, outside the original sample you used to estimate it. Thus, going forward, the *odds* will likely perform slightly worse than backtests suggest, and the *evens* will perform slightly better. It is easy to anticipate out-of-sample decay in this case because you *know* that the length of a company's name is unlikely to affect performance. However, this same logic could apply to a number of screens that you end up using, which you think are meaningful, but actually are not.

Incidentally, there is a way to simulate the out-of-sample decay. If you construct a screen backtesting with data only up to 2012, and you run the screen from 2012 to present once you have finalized it, you will gain some sense of the out-of-sample decay, without having to run the screen in real life. This technique is known as using a *hold-out sample*. The idea is that you are holding out some of the data when constructing your screen and then, once you have created a model using your base sample, you can test the model on the hold-out sample. It is used widely in measuring out-of-sample model effectiveness.

Finally, as mentioned, you will lose whatever transaction costs you incur and these will erode your realized returns. That being said, if you can estimate them, you can actually simulate the drag in backtests that you perform in Equities Lab (or in other pieces of software).

Suppose you run your strategy and find it does not work. Perhaps your results look nothing like those in backtests, and you are losing money hand over fist. In such a case, I recommend you skip ahead to the section titled "What If My Quantitative Strategy Stops Working?" in Chapter 16, "Why Does Quantitative Investing Work?" and seek solace there.

Role of Quantitative Equity Investing in Overall Wealth Management

The role of quantitative equity investing in your overall wealth management process is likely to be very person-specific. This section gives a rough idea of how it would look for a typical reader of this book, but everyone's situation is different.

First, take a look at Figure 14.3, which proposes a relatively aggressive asset allocation profile over the years for a hypothetical Mr. Aggro.

This allocation covers liquid assets and does not include retirement accounts and real estate. Putting some net worth numbers on the chart, suppose that Mr. Aggro's liquid net worth was about $25,000 in his twenties, and he would put $20,000 in equities (all U.S.)

keeping $5,000 against unexpected expenses. It is likely Mr. Aggro would also be able to seek his parents' help if his investments fail, so this is fine.

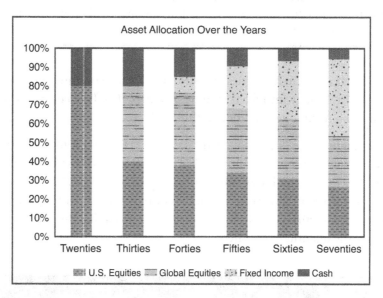

Figure 14.3 Asset allocation by age for a hypothetical aggressive investor, Mr. Aggro

At this stage of life, it is perfectly reasonable to put the entire $20,000 in quantitative U.S. equity strategies. Mr. Aggro has all the time in the world, and unless he is planning to buy a house soon, or has some other major planned expense, he can just let it ride.

In his thirties, forties, and fifties, the fixed income portion of his liquid net worth steadily increases. Additionally, Mr. Aggro decides to equally diversify his equity port-folio between global and U.S. equities. Assuming net worth of $75,000, $130,000, and $220,000 in these decades, the U.S. equities portion amounts to $30,000, $50,000, and $75,000 in these decades. The global equities constitute a similar amount. Quantitative techniques can be used to manage as much (or as little) of this allocation as desired. If Mr. Aggro has tools to do quantitative investing among global equities, he could also manage that allocation using quantitative techniques.[8]

TIP

Retirement accounts may be a particularly profitable place to deploy safer quantita-tive strategies. In particular, tax-free accounts, such as Traditional and Roth IRAs, work particularly well because neither dividends nor short-term capital gains incur a bill from Uncle Sam. However, a number of retirement accounts (such as 401ks) do not have freedom to trade in equities. Also, because transaction costs generally have to be paid from the tax-advantage funds, it is wasteful to expend this source of funds for commissions. Thus, if you can create a long rebalance period strategy and implement in a low transaction cost account, go for it. Otherwise, stick to a low-cost ETF in retirement accounts.

As Mr. Aggro gets older, in his sixties and seventies, he also becomes more cautious and moves more of his money into fixed income products. The U.S. equity portion can still be managed using techniques outlined in this book.

What would quantitative equity investing have done for Mr. Aggro over his lifetime? Assume he only used it for managing half of his U.S. equity portfolio and the outperformance of this versus the index was a conservative 5% a year.[9] This would lead to a lifetime annual outperformance of 1.5% on his entire net worth, or roughly doubling Mr. Aggro's net worth at retirement. This is no mean feat, given that this arose from a limited deployment of the quantitative strategies.

TIP

The old adage for asset allocation between equities and fixed income used to be, put 100-minus-your-age percent in equities. So if you are 25 years old, you'd put 75% in equities. Of course, with decreasing interest rates, the sense is that this is overly cautious and will not yield enough to provide return in savings. Allocations such as Mr. Aggro's are becoming more common.

Endnotes

1. Transferring money between brokerage accounts is onerous, as you need to reconcile cost bases, and it complicates tax accounting for the year the transfer occurs because you'll receive forms from both brokerages. It's still worth doing for the right reasons. That being said, if you're creating a new brokerage account, there's no reason not to do it with the "best" brokerage for your particular situation.

2. There are two different types of margin: daily margin (you can buy up to four times the amount of value in your account, as long as you sell positions before day's end), and longer-term margin, which is typically two times the value of the account. If you end a day in a situation where your positions are more than two times the value of your account, you will have a margin call, which will hurt. The

brokerage will randomly sell positions until your position to account value ratio drops below two. This is particularly troublesome if the brokerage decides to sell an illiquid position, where selling further exacerbates your loss by incurring needless transaction costs. It is also troublesome if the brokerage sells a position with a gain, triggering a needless tax event.

3. By discount broker, I'm referring to the slew of brokerages that charge $6.99 or $9.99 or some similar "low" number per trade. There are even discount brokers that have started offering free transactions, subject to certain conditions. For example, Merrill Lynch's brokerage offers a fixed number of free transactions per month if you have a certain level of assets with Bank of America (Bank of America acquired Merrill Lynch during the financial crisis). Another brokerage, Robin Hood, offers free trades to beta testers, but you have to trade on their mobile app platform.

4. This is a variant of "A Defensive Screen," described in Chapter 10, "Some Powerful Screens."

5. 200% returns over ten years can be generated by 11.6% per year ($3^{1/10} = 1.116$). Similarly, 75% returns over ten years are generated by 5.7% per year. The difference, about 6%, is what we expected the strategy to outperform by annually. Of course, in reality, there will be some years in which outperformance is more, and others in which it is less.

6. The catch here is that you have to trade on a phone or tablet. This might make trading a basket of 20 or 30 stocks a bit cumbersome.

7. The expense ratio is the fee the fund manager charges for the money he or she manages. Cheap funds have expense ratios as low or lower than 0.10% of assets. That means that if you put $1,000 into a fund with a 0.10% expense ratio, each year, the manager of the fund would take $1 ($1,000 × 0.10% = $1) as a fee. The typical value ETF will charge about 0.40% of assets.

8. Equities Lab currently only analyzes U.S. equities. American Depository Receipts (ADRs) are included, so that is one way to use Equities Lab to invest in foreign stocks. However, to invest directly in foreign stocks, an alternative data source, such as Bloomberg, is needed.

9. Also assume all other portions of his liquid net worth were put in cheap index funds (or checking accounts in the bank for cash).

15

Alternative Tools for Quantitative Investing

By now, you are probably quite comfortable with Equities Lab. However, this book only comes with 20 weeks of Equities Lab. After that, you will have to pay for a subscription, albeit at a discounted rate. However, it is possible that you will not want to pay for Equities Lab after the trial ends. Or perhaps you need to do some quantitative analysis that is not currently supported by Equities Lab.

In this case, you need an alternative tool to do your quantitative investing. The most flexible alternative investing tool is a database of stock returns and characteristics you want to analyze, along with the coding chops to conduct screens and backtests.

For those of you who are students, there are educational databases of stock returns and accounting data that are relatively affordable, or possibly even freely available at your educational institution. The most common among these are CRSP (data from the Center for Research in Security Prices) and Compustat. You can merge CRSP and Compustat databases and have the basic building block of a data set much like the one behind Equities Lab. Unfortunately, the academic databases often have a delay to them. For example, the most recent data may be from a quarter or two ago. This might not ordinarily be an issue for backtests, but for screening stocks to hold in a portfolio today, this might prove an insurmountable barrier. Alternatively, access to up-to-date data sources solves this problem.

Many sophisticated quantitative investors, such as hedge fund managers, often collect data themselves. If you believe that there is some unique data that is particularly predictive regarding future stock prices, you must collect the data yourself and create a merged data set with stock returns to backtest your strategy. Additionally, you need some way to collect the data you need in real time.[1]

Comparing Equities Lab to Other Analysis Platforms (With Contributions from Henry Crutcher, Founder and CEO of Equities Lab)

If you do not find merging data sets and coding to your taste, other alternative analysis tools are out there. I have tried some of them. Others, I have read about. I am not an expert in all the analytical tools in the marketplace. However, I will say that, in terms of bang for your buck, Equities Lab is pretty far up there. In addition to reviewing my experience with some other analytical tools in market, the following section also draws heavily on Henry Crutcher's opinions on some of Equities Lab's competitors. I am grateful to him for providing his analysis (but in the interests of full disclosure, Crutcher is the founder and CEO of Equities Lab, so these companies are his competition). If you see a tool that interests you, do some research to decide if it will work for you and your individual situation.

Bloomberg

Bloomberg provides much more data than Equities Lab. Bloomberg has pricing information for everything under the sun, whereas Equities Lab only has information on U.S. equities. You can screen stocks according to a variety of criteria, built-in or custom, in both Bloomberg and Equities Lab. Also, you can backtest trading strategies easily and quickly. (Equities Lab is generally a bit quicker than the average Bloomberg backtest, but that might change if Equities Lab's server load grows to rival theirs.) Bloomberg terminals are expensive and are not in common use by individuals. (They cost $20K–30K per year.)

Compustat/Capital IQ

Compustat is well regarded by the professional investment community. It also has a screening and backtesting product (ClariFi) that does pretty much everything Equities Lab does, and possibly more. However, each number presented by Capital IQ has been adjusted in some way to make it more "consistent." This prevents you from using actual values filed with the SEC for analysis because they do not keep preadjustment values. Also, like Bloomberg, it is expensive, and it is rare to find individual investors using Capital IQ. (It runs in the tens of thousands per year, depending on what exact services you purchase.)

YCharts

YCharts charts any stock and a variety of fundamental indicators and macroeconomic data about the stock. Equities Lab is similar, except that you can use your own indicators (fundamental, technical, or macroeconomic) of arbitrary complexity. Equities Lab plots average values of indicators over a basket of stocks. YCharts does not have this amount of flexibility. YCharts runs about $2,500 per year, and only plots stock charts. It will not do backtests of screens.

Portfolio123

Portfolio123 uses a subset of Compustat data (about 78 fields worth from the balance sheet, quoting their line item reference, versus the 700 or so that Morningstar provides). Again, recall that Compustat data is adjusted to shield investors from the messy world out there, which is good for simplicity, but could be bad for deep analysis. Their backtest results yield a chart and the underlying data, but they are not interactive (which is understandable given that they run in a browser). Portfolio123 runs $1,000 per year for a system that lets you backtest up to 1999. It is probably the most direct competitor to Equities Lab.

Stock Investor Pro

Stock Investor Pro is a gold-standard stock screener. However, Stock Investor Pro has no backtest, no charting, no technical analysis, limited custom formulas, and limited, potentially unreliable data. Stock Investor 3 runs on Windows only, and costs about $200 per year.

VectorVest

VectorVest offers advice and screens that describe which stocks to buy. VectorVest also lets you screen stocks in the past. However, VectorVest only lets you screen on a handful of proprietary indicators and a few technical analysis indicators. It does not screen on accounting data released by companies. The plan that has the bulk of their features runs $645 per year.

StockCharts.com

StockCharts.com plots a variety of technical indicators and charts them. It also plots these charts in a variety of appealing formats, with volume bars, point and figure charts, and more. StockCharts.com does not plot fundamental indicators, macroeconomic indicators, or custom indicators, whereas Equities Lab does. The middle-of-the-road version of StockCharts.com costs $250 per year.

Stock Rover

Stock Rover is another screening and portfolio management tool. The scope of screening is a bit more limited than Equities Lab (for example, it cannot describe complicated conditions, such as "Price has made its first new high within the last year" or "Earnings were going up over the last 20 quarters, then they started going down"). Also, and this is a deal breaker, when they describe and report returns, they do so given *current* holdings. So all you know about a portfolio is that it picks stocks that have already done well. Put another way, it is impossible to meaningfully backtest a trading strategy. This lack of an ability to "screen in the past" prevents you from validating your idea. The premium version of Stock Rover runs $250 per year.

Finviz

Finviz (finviz comes from a portmanteau of *financial* and *visualization*) focuses on creating visual representations of the investment space. Like Equities Lab, it has appealing charts and a heat map. Their screener is limited to a collection of pull-downs, and their backtest lets you backtest one security at a time. Finviz has a nice free offering, and their elite service is $400 per year. They have a potentially useful further listing of various services, mostly oriented toward technical analysis and day traders.

Newsletters

These are among the most common investing tool. Newsletters that provide analysis on stocks are often underpinned by quantitative analysis from software such as Bloomberg or Portfolio 123. The advantage of generating results directly from software is that you can customize analysis to meet your needs, and see how changing screens changes suggested holdings and backtest results. Navalier ($500 per year) and fool.com (average $200 per year) both have quantitative strategies that underpin their newsletters.

The upshot is that there are a variety of financial tools out there. Equities Lab is one that is particularly well-suited for the type of quantitative investing described in this book, and is thus the focus of analysis in this book. However, you should use the best tool available.

Endnotes

1. During the dot-com bubble of the late nineties, a popular quant strategy was to check what stocks would be featured on CNBC in advance and to just buy them. The sentiment among day traders was so bullish that often the simple act of being covered by CNBC would lead to a small pop during the airing.

16

Why Does Quantitative Investing Work?

Now that you have learned all about quantitative investing, let me take a step back. The standard disclosure on most financial services products (including mutual funds and other investment advisory services) almost always includes the phrase "Past performance may not be indicative of future performance." So why, then, do I promote an investing style, which by its very nature, relies on backtesting to validate ideas?

First, before detailing the case against quantitative investing, let me posit that backtesting is a small part of quantitative investing. As discussed in the section, "The Problem with Building Strategies Solely to Outperform in Backtests," in Chapter 3, "Creating a Screen—The Nuts and Bolts of Choosing a Quantitative Investing Strategy," you can build strategies solely to maximize backtest results, but doing that is probably not going to produce the desired results. Instead, recall that you need to have some purpose when you design your screen beyond simply maximizing backtest results. That being said, much of the appeal of quantitative strategies comes from backtests, and we need to address the concern that past patterns might not continue into the future.

The Case Against Quantitative Investing

The main case against quantitative investing relies on a paradoxical piece of financial academic theory, the *efficient markets hypothesis*. This hypothesis states that markets should be informationally efficient, or that prices should reflect all available information.[1] Any outperforming strategy in terms of returns has to be the result of some additional risk that the strategy is bearing. The underpinnings of this theory are the fact that if the price of a stock ever diverged from its "true value," thousands of investors would buy or sell the security until the price was consistent with the true value. Of course, this last part is paradoxical. These investors who swoop in to take advantage of mispriced securities are themselves trading in an inefficient market, although their trades make the market efficient.

A natural consequence of the efficient markets hypothesis is that no screen should be able to deliver returns that significantly beat the market. This is the basis of the most common financial advice experts dole out: "Invest in cheap index funds or exchange traded funds (ETFs)." There are far worse pieces of advice than this and for investors of limited means (either monetary or temporal), this is a prudent approach.

Why It Still Works

So given all the academic theory and common sense that urges against quantitative techniques, why does it still work? There are three principal explanations for the success of quantitative investing strategies, as discussed in the following sections.

Fair Reward for Additional Risk

The first explanation relies on the fact that the efficient markets hypothesis leaves us an escape route: Namely, strategies can generate excess returns *if* they also carry with them some added risk. The most famous of these is likely to be a strategy that levers up on market risk. Chapter 2, "What You Need to Start Investing Using Quantitative Techniques," discussed this concept briefly in the breakout on market beta in the section, "Results Explained."

The idea here is that the market outperforms the risk-free rate in expectation because investing in the market is risky, and investors need additional compensation to bear that risk. Pushing this logic further, investing in stocks that are especially sensitive to the market (or those with higher *betas*) should carry even higher expected returns than the market, but this outperformance comes at the cost of greater market sensitivity. This means that when the market goes up, these stocks go up more, and when the market goes down, they go down more. In other words, when the world is economically sound (and you don't particularly need money from investments), you're making money, and when the world is economically depressed (and when you need money from investments), you're losing money. Thus, the added expected return for these stocks is compensation for the ill-timed payoffs and penalties.

In Figure 16.1, you can see that stocks that are more sensitive to the market (1 < beta < 2) outperform those less sensitive to the market (0 < beta < 1) by about 50%–60% over ten years.[2]

Figure 16.1 Backtest of 0 < beta < 1 (top) and 1 < beta < 2 (bottom) (weekly rebalance, no other conditions)

In this case, it is easy to identify the added risk that leads to the added returns. In other cases, such as the outperformance of value stocks, it is harder to see what risks are associated with those stocks. That being said, a number of academics have made attempts. For example, in "The Value Premium," Lu Zhang argues that because value stocks already have assets in place (high book value, relative to price), they carry the risk of not being easily redeployed as a result of business shocks (2005). In contrast, growth stocks (the opposite of value stocks) tend to be more flexible and are better at coping with changes in the business environment.

Similarly, academics have proposed risk-based explanations for a number of factors that predict future returns.[3] Aside from the market risk premium (documented previously), there is relatively little consensus on whether a given predictive marker is an anomaly or a priced risk factor.[4] Regardless, this view of quantitative investing can be either reassuring or concerning. It is reassuring because it suggests there is a concrete reason why certain screens outperform. It is concerning because there are added risks to these screens that justify the added returns. In some sense, if you are investing for the very long run (10+ years), the added returns are probably well worth the added risk. Put another way, if financial experts are comfortable advising young people to invest in stocks (as opposed to bonds), they should similarly be comfortable advising people to invest in other outperforming sectors (such as value, momentum, and so forth), even if the outperformance results from additional risk.

Behavioral Explanations

A second explanation of why quantitative investing works involves behavioral biases. Behavioral biases are behaviors that need not be return-maximizing but make the investor happy or psychologically comfortable in some other way. Remember the behavioral biases discussed and avoided by investing using quantitative techniques (see Chapter 13, "Behavioral Biases Avoided by Investing Quantitatively")? One way to make money is by taking advantage of all the other traders out there who are not investing using these techniques and are susceptible to behavioral biases.

One example involves the higher returns that investors receive for holding value stocks. Value stocks are stocks with a low PE. The opposite, growth stocks, are stocks with a high PE (or high price to book), or even stocks with negative earnings. Growth stocks are likely to be stocks that are mentioned in the news. Stocks such as Facebook, Twitter, Amazon, and Netflix are all growth stocks and have PE ratios significantly above the average PE ratio for the market as a whole. Behavioral explanations of this premium abound. For example, people invested in growth stocks might want to hold them so that they can talk about them at cocktail parties, and so that they feel competent (or even clever) when they read media pieces on these stocks (which are far more frequent than media pieces on value stocks).

A story along these lines is proposed by Deniz Anginer and Meir Statman in "Stocks of Admired Companies and Spurned Ones," where they show that holding stocks in "admired" companies according to *Fortune Magazine*'s list of America's Most Admired Companies generally lags the performance of "spurned" companies, which have a lower rating on the admired companies list (2010).

Differentiating between a risk-based and behavioral explanation for anomalies has proven to be a fertile topic for discussion in academic and media circles. The outperformance of value, for example, has been analyzed in "Contrarian Investment, Extrapolation, and Risk" to tease out whether the outperformance is driven by risk-based or behavioral reasons (Lakonishok, Shleifer, & Vishny, 1994).

This behavioral explanation for the outperformance of quantitative strategies is the dream explanation for the quantitative investors. It seems unlikely that investors prone to behavioral biases as a whole will change their preference for holding stocks that they enjoy talking about with their friends and reading about in the news. As such, a quantitative investor, who presumably is not motivated by such pleasures, will buy the stocks largely ignored by behavioral investors, and at cheaper prices (because these stocks don't have as much demand for them), reaping higher returns.

Rewards for Making Markets Efficient

The third and final explanation for why quantitative investing works is because quantitative investors *are* the investors swooping in and taking advantage of inefficiencies. In the process, they make some money and make markets efficient. This is what a working paper by David McLean and Jeff Pontiff, "Does Academic Research Destroy Stock Return Predictability?" argues. They study a number of published anomalies (anomalies are simply quantitative strategies that have done well in backtests over very long periods) and show that after publication, there is a decline in the profitability of the strategy over time (2014).

In reality, the mechanism by which strategies disappear is a bit more interesting. For example, imagine that a profitable strategy, such as value investing, or high F-score investing, is an anomaly and that there is no reasonable basis for the outperformance to continue. What happens? A bunch of savvy quantitative investors (like you) pile in. In the short run, as more investors pile in, the returns to the strategy increase spectacularly, before the strategy is fairly priced and no longer generates outperforming returns.

This means that many of these strategies actually follow a "supernova" type pattern, where the returns steadily improve as more and more investors pile in, and then when the underlying stocks are fairly valued, the screens stop generating abnormal returns, or very few stocks fulfill the criteria. For example, in a value strategy, the underlying stocks would be fairly valued when most stocks reach high enough PE levels that the screen does not select them.

This explanation is particularly concerning to quantitative investors. At some level, it's reassuring to know that the high returns to screens are actually the results of making a market efficient. However, the concerning part is that it's never clear (except long, long after the fact) when a strategy has stopped working. This is the subject of the final section in this chapter.

What If My Quantitative Strategy Stops Working?

Imagine that you've lost a fair bit of your portfolio and you are wondering whether the strategy that you've chosen is fundamentally flawed. Or even worse, you might be wondering if quantitative investing itself is fundamentally flawed. Let me reassure you about the second concern first. Quantitative investing will outlive us all. There will always be quantitative investors in all asset classes where data is relatively easily available and transaction costs are relatively low. There are, of course, asset classes where quantitative investing doesn't work particularly well. For example, in direct residential real estate investment, where transaction costs are high, quantitative techniques are probably ill-suited. If U.S. equities ever evolve in this direction, perhaps due to rising transaction costs and data becoming unavailable, quantitative techniques may no longer be as applicable to U.S. equity investing. However, this seems unlikely.

The first concern is more worrying. You've found an elegant strategy that meets your objective and produces solid backtest results. Maybe the strategy has already performed well for a while. Maybe you've just launched it. Recently, however, you have started to lose large sums of money while following the strategy. You are beginning to wonder if the strategy has stopped working. How can you distinguish a run of bad luck from the death of a quantitative strategy?

Answering this question is more of an art than a science. First, let's eliminate two potential types of losses. First, if your strategy is not well diversified (maybe you only have three holdings in your quantitative strategy), it's perfectly possible for one stock to plummet, leading to a large percentage loss on your overall quantitative portfolio. Incidentally, it's equally likely that you hit the jackpot on one of these positions and realize a wonderful return. Although I hope you experience the latter, both of these outcomes are essentially driven by luck, and it would not be legitimate to attribute the results to the quantitative system you are using.

The second type of loss is the short-term small loss. You have lost 5%–10% over the last two weeks. You are still in the black because your portfolio had gained that 10% over the course of the last year, but now you are petrified and want to pull all your money out of this whimsical quantitative system and put it back under your mattress before you actually lose money. This reaction is understandable, but this is exactly what quantitative systems are designed to prevent you from doing. Remember that one of the drivers of quantitative investments is behavioral bias, including the fear of losses.[5] Stay the course. In fact, it might be prudent to avoid looking at your portfolio at all in between rebalancing periods. Trading based on these short-term swings essentially negates the potential power of whatever strategy you had, and you end up no better off than the speculators who buy stocks based on what they see in the news or recent performance.

The third and last type of loss—a long, persistent string of losses in a strategy over an extended period of time—is the true worry. To figure out if something is wrong with your strategy, first consider how other strategies are doing. Is the market as a whole losing money during this period? Very few quantitative strategies made money during the financial crisis of 2008. However, many quantitative strategies helped their investors avoid the worst of that awful year and ended the year with losses far lower than the 38% loss suffered by the S&P 500. In these cases, I would not be too worried unless you need the money in your account in the short term. In that case, you probably should not be investing in equities to begin with, so withdraw your money, lick your wounds, and try again when you have the capital to stay the course through market turbulence.

However, if your strategy is uniquely underperforming other strategies and the market as a whole has been doing so for a year or more, it might be worth analyzing *why* it is underperforming. If the underperformance is the result of a single sector or industry that suffered a shock, you could reduce the volatility around the strategy by limiting exposure to any single industry, or excluding that industry from your screens. If the underperformance is diffuse and spread over all your names and doesn't seem to have any discernable pattern, you might want to consider moving on to a different screen. That being said, even the most popular and robust screens sometimes have two to three bad years in a row followed by a significant turnaround. If you pull out before that even-tual turnaround, you could end up missing out on an eventual recovery.

Ultimately, I have no idea whether that one- to two-year underperformance of your strategy is bad luck or the end of your strategy's useful life. I am sure you will come up with some rules by which to judge these matters, and I encourage you to contact me to share the rules you devise.

Endnotes

1. In fact, there are a number of forms of this hypothesis. They range from forms where current prices simply reflect historical price information to forms where prices reflect even insider information. Eugene Fama detailed this in his paper "Efficient Capital Markets: A Review of Theory and Empirical Work" (1970). Most forms of efficiency would suggest any screens based on public data should not be able to outperform.

2. The actual magnitude of the outperformance also lines up with the idea of the market risk premium discussed in Chapter 7, endnote 6. The higher beta stocks have an average beta (1.4) that is 0.8 higher than the lower beta stocks (0.6). Per

year, the outperformance should be 6% (the market risk premium) × 0.8 (the increased beta) = 4.8%. Compounding that over ten years, you get the 50%–60% outperformance.

3. In academic papers, something observable today that predicts future returns is known as an *anomaly*. If that something is correlated with a source of priced risk as well, such as market betas, it becomes a *risk factor*. In a working paper arguing that current academic tests to determine anomalies and risk factors are too lenient, Harvey, Liu, and Zhu posit that there are currently (as of 2014), 314 anomalies (Harvey, Liu, & Zhu, 2014).

4. Recall that an anomaly is a variable that predicts future stock returns, and a priced risk factor is a variable that predicts future stocks returns but is also tied to some additional risk, which in turn warrants the additional return generated.

5. Kahneman and Tversky describe this bias as *loss aversion* in their Nobel Prize winning work, "Prospect Theory: An Analysis of Decision Under Risk" (1979). They also document a number of other behavioral biases in the paper, which are worth reading. Chapter 13 covers some of these biases briefly.

17

Quantitative Investing in the Markets Today

Now that you have a sense of the purpose and power of quantitative investing and have perhaps created and backtested some strategies yourself, this chapter briefly discusses the evolution of quantitative investing, and, more important, the competitive landscape for quantitative investors in today's market. This chapter is not designed to discourage, but to inform. The more quantitative traders there are, the more it means that there truly is something behind the techniques outlined in this book. On the other hand, it also means there are more people out there pursuing similar techniques, and any edge you acquire from following the quant techniques in this book are diminishing.

A Brief History of Quantitative Investing

For much of its existence, quantitative investing has been the exclusive privilege of big banks, well-heeled hedge funds, and other large institutional investors. The reasons for this are that until very recently, quantitative investing required both cutting-edge technology and access to the latest, and often very expensive, data. Although the exclusivity of such practices still exists within quantitative trading—high-frequency traders often spend vast sums of money to shed nanoseconds from their trades—recent developments (including this book and tools such as Equities Lab) have opened up quantitative investing to the individual, retail, and small institutional investors.

It is important to take a moment to examine the history of quantitative finance to best understand where we are now and where we may be headed in the future.[1]

The history of modern quantitative finance is largely a story of ideas moving from obscurity to ever-increasing accessibility. What once existed purely in the realm of obscure mathematicians or natural scientists would come to be at the heart of mainstream financial academics. While quantitative investing would produce some of the most successful and dominant strategies in recent history, its origins go back to the turn of the century. Applying mathematics to finance is a relatively new practice; however, the foundation for doing such is much older. Many consider the founding fathers of quantitative finance to be two French academics, Louis Bachelier and (Polish-born) Benoit Mandelbrot. Their work would prove to be essential in the development of quantitative finance, although the importance of their work was initially overlooked. Bachelier is widely considered to be the first person to broadly publish on the subject of using complicated mathematical models to price and analyze the world of finance in practical terms. He did so most famously as part of his PhD thesis titled *The Theory of Speculation* (Bachelier, 1900). In this paper, he discussed a phenomenon known as *Brownian motion*. Brownian motion is named after the botanist Robert Brown, who in 1827 noticed pollen particles he was examining moved in a jerky, unpredictable way. The movement of these particles defied pattern and appeared to be following a random path. Bachelier's paper suggested that stocks and options moved in a similarly random way.

This understanding of the market, one filled with a series of individual stocks that on their own move in a fundamentally and mathematically indeterminable direction, would come to serve as a basis for quantitatively minded academics and investors. This work, while important, went largely ignored by Bachelier's contemporaries in the field of finance. Over half a century later, Mandelbrot, a mathematician by training who is also known in the field as the father of fractal geometry, used statistical analysis to further push the idea that a market performing properly would be one in which the movements of its individual elements would be unpredictable. In the eyes of many theorists, these works helped cement the idea that the market is composed of a series of "random walks." This idea, according to Bachelier and Mandelbrot, essentially meant that at any time, any individual stock is just as likely to go up as it is to go down.

While academics were pondering the mathematical models that could explore stock prices, trading in stocks in this era was largely a loud, chaotic affair. Scenes from movies with traders yelling in the trading pit characterized much of the action. A good trader had good instincts, intuitively knowing what the tenor of the frenzy suggested about the future, and having the nerve to risk financial ruin to emerge richer than before.

It would be several years before Bachelier and Mandelbrot's idea of the unpredictability of stock prices began to take root, even among academics. The work of academics such as Eugene Fama, along with others, transformed what had been an intellectual exploration into one with real-world implications. Fama's famous 1970 paper, "Efficient Capital Markets: A Review of Theory and Empirical Work," offered an expanded explanation of the market's "random walk." The paper also set the stage for a refrain that continues today: Stock prices are efficient. There is no way to beat the market. Invest in a cheap mutual fund to capture the wonderful financial benefits the broad market offers.

However, there were heretics, both in academic circles as well as among practitioners, who noticed that certain types of stocks outperformed. The ultimate irony is that ultimately, Fama himself, along with Kenneth French, published another seminal piece, "The Cross-Section of Expected Stock Returns," which documented the outperformance of certain segments of the stock market relative to others (1992). Around this time, there was also a growing group of economists suggesting there were behavioral biases that were *systematically* affecting stock prices. And in the background, away from the publicly available academic journal articles, practitioners continued minting money based on relationships that they discerned to predict future stock prices.

In to the nineties and the aughts, increasingly cheaper and easier access to data, computing, and telecommunications led to increasing amounts of quantitative investing, and even more quantitative trading. Many high-frequency trading shops started, some to provide liquidity to other traders, but some others to take advantage of loopholes in the rules of exchanges and other trading venues.[2] In parallel, behemoth hedge funds developed around quantitative investing strategies (some of which are described in this book).

These funds, often backed by deep-pocketed investors or large banks, were able to create investment strategies that produced unprecedented returns both in terms of their magnitude and reliability. Firms such as Renaissance Technologies, Citadel, Robeco, and AQR became the talk of the street posting staggering profits year after year. As the techniques spread, mutual funds, ETFs, and other long-only investors started deploying capital according to these quantitative algorithms, and these strategies finally become accessible to retail investors. In the recent decade, these quantitatively based funds (often called *smart beta* funds) have taken off like a rocket, and quantitatively oriented ETFs alone managed $350 billion in 2014, growing at a 30% clip.[3] Together with the quantitatively run mutual funds, hedge funds, and other institutional investors, these strategies now account for more money than ever.

Finally, we are at a point in the story where data, know-how, and implementation have become so cheap that it is possible to apply quantitative investing techniques directly at the retail level. We have reached the point where you, armed with this book, Equities Lab, and a brokerage account, can create and execute a quantitative strategy that will hold its own in the markets. It's unclear how this story ends, but I do know that quantitative equity investing with retail levels of capital, retail levels of know-how, and retail levels of data is now possible. And that's a big deal.

How Can You Compete Against Billion-Dollar Hedge Fund Behemoths?

Reading the previous section might have diminished your enthusiasm for the phenomenal quant strategy you created using Equities Lab. You might be wondering, "How can I possibly compete against hedge funds and mutual funds with billions of dollars, who are hiring teams of people for millions of dollars to come up with powerful quantitative strategies?"

The good news is that you may not need to because of two things: First, there's more than enough to go around for everyone. You want to buy value stocks rather than growth stocks? Go for it—as long as some investors are still drawn to the razzle-dazzle of growth stocks, some version of the value premium will continue. Want to trade momentum? Again, go for it. It is crash prone, but as long as you understand the added risk you're taking, and have a long enough horizon to weather any short-term storms, you should be fine.

Second, as a small, retail investor, there are places in the investable universe where you can invest where larger investors cannot. In particular, small cap stocks are generally shunned by larger investors, as well as by many financial advisors.

Larger investors shun small caps simply because they cannot invest enough money in them. For example, Fidelity's Magellan fund has about $17 billion in assets. If it were to look in the $100–$250 million market cap space, it could not reasonably deploy even half a percent of assets in each company it found attractive without buying half of the company. If it were to buy half the company, it would bid up prices, and then have to be intimately involved in operations—because it would effectively become the owner to the firm. Thus, these larger investors are limited to large cap stocks and often avoid the small cap space.

Many financial advisors dislike small cap stocks because they are unknown. Put differently: If I, as a financial advisor, told a client to invest in Apple, and it went down 20% or 30%, I could talk my way out of it, appealing to the fact that a bunch of other investors also thought it was great and now everyone is suffering through the loss. If, instead, I told my client to invest in a no-name small cap stock and it lost 20% to 30%, I'd probably lose my client.[4]

This dislike for small caps makes quantitative strategies in this space particularly appealing for the retail investor. However, small size and illiquidity often come hand in hand, so I would urge any investors in this space to be cognizant of the added transaction costs associated with these names.[5]

At the end of the day, investing money with one of the big institutions that uses quantitative strategies may be perfectly appropriate, especially if you do not like doing the kind of analysis described in this book, and trading stocks directly in your brokerage account is stressful for you. This just leads to some of the problems covered in Chapter 14, "How Do You Actually Make Money Now? A Brief Guide to Implementation," in the section, "Quantitative Investing If You Are Limited to ETFs and Mutual Funds." Fees and the lack of control of the strategy are among two of the big drawbacks of outsourcing fund management.

If, instead, you do decide to enter the exciting world of quantitative equity investing, welcome. The water's warm and there's plenty of room in the pool.

Endnotes

1. Although I try to cover some of the highlights of the history of quantitative investing, I strongly recommend the book, *The Quants* by Scott Patterson (2010) for a more comprehensive treatment of the subject—and an entertaining read.

2. See *Dark Pools: The Rise of the Machine Traders and the Rigging of the U.S. Stock Market* for details (Patterson, 2012). High-frequency trading is certainly quantitative in nature, with a strategy, backtests, and implementation concerns. However, given its very short horizon and technological requirements, it is beyond the scope of this book. Besides, with holding periods in the sub-second range, and a general preference to zero out positions before close of markets, it hardly qualifies as quantitative "investing."

3. See Balchunas (2014).

4. If you are an advisor who avoids the small cap space, I urge you to reconsider; with quantitative investing techniques backing you up, you will no longer be investing in a no-name $50 million market cap stock. Rather, you will be investing in an academically documented strategy, backed with recent empirical evidence. That should hopefully be defensible to your clients.

5. The standard Restrictions tab I propose excludes small cap names. If you do decide to include some of the smaller cap companies in your screens, be sure to appropriately compromise by imposing a higher penalty for transaction costs.

18

Godspeed

As we wrap up this primer on quantitative equity investing, I would like to wish you all the best in your investing endeavors. Quantitative investing is a fantastic method of investing, and many of the techniques discussed in this book can be applied to investments outside of U.S. equities. I hope you find these techniques as useful as I did, and that this book and Equities Lab have helped get you up and running on your quantitative investing agenda.

I leave you with some words of wisdom from an academic and an investor. Both quotes are somewhat applicable to the field of quantitative investing:

> *"Investing should be more like watching paint dry or watching grass grow.*
> *If you want excitement, take $800 and go to Las Vegas."*
>
> —Paul Samuelson

> *"The four most dangerous words in investing are: 'this time it's different.'"*
>
> —Sir John Templeton

And finally, as a congratulatory note for reaching the end of the book, a word from my favorite Founding Father...

> *"An investment in knowledge pays the best interest."*
>
> —Benjamin Franklin

Bibliography

Anginer, D., & Statman, M. (2010, Spring). Stocks of admired companies and spurned ones. *Journal of Portfolio Management, 36*(3), 71–77.

Asness, C. S., Frazzini, A., Israel, R., & Moskowitz, T. J. (2014). Fact, fiction, and momentum investing. *Journal of Portfolio Management, 40*(5), 60–67.

Asness, C. S., Moskowitz, T. J., & Pedersen, L. H. (2013, June). Value and momentum everywhere. *The Journal of Finance, 68*(3), 929–985.

Bachelier, L. (1900). *The theory of speculation* (Doctoral dissertation). Retrieved from http://www.jstor.org/stable/j.ctt7scn4. (Access to jstor required.)

Balchunas, E. (2014, August 27). Smart Beta: The Investing Buzzword That Won't—and Needn't—Die. *Bloomberg Business.*

Barberis, N., & Xiong, W. (2009, April). What drives the disposition effect? An analysis of a long-standing preference-based explanation. *The Journal of Finance, 64*(2), 751–784.

Carhart, M. M. (1997, March). On persistence in mutual fund performance. *The Journal of Finance, 52*(1), 57–82.

Conrad, J., Gultekin, M. N., & Kaul, G. (1997). Profitability of short-term contrarian strategies: Implications for market efficiency. *Journal of Business & Economic Statistics, 15*(3), 379–386.

Fama, E. F. (1970, May). Efficient capital markets: A review of theory and empirical work. *The Journal of Finance, 25*(2), 383–417.

Fama, E. F., & French, K. R. (1992, June). The cross-section of expected stock returns. *The Journal of Finance, 47*(2), 427–465.

Graham, B. (1976, September/October). A conversation with Benjamin Graham. *Financial Analysts Journal, 32*(5), 20–23.

Graham, B., & Dodd, D. (1934). *Security analysis.* McGraw-Hill.

Gray, W. R., & Carlisle, T. E. (2012). *Quantitative value.* Wiley.

Greenblatt, J. (2005). *The little book that beats the market.* John Wiley & Sons.

Harvey, C., Liu, Y., & Zhu, H. (2014). ...and the cross-section of expected returns (Working Paper).

Horowitz, J. L., Loughran, T., & Savin, N. E. (2000, August). Three analyses of the firm size premium. *Journal of Empirical Finance, 7*(2), 143–153.

Jegadeesh, N., & Titman, S. (1993, March). Returns to buying winners and selling losers: Implications for stock market efficiency. *The Journal of Finance, 48*(1), 65–91.

Kahneman, D., & Tversky, A. (1979, March). Prospect theory: An analysis of decision under risk. *Econometrica, 47*(2), 263–292.

Kang, J., Liu, M.-H., & Ni, S. X. (2002, June). Contrarian and momentum strategies in the China stock market: 1993–2000. *Pacific-Basin Finance Journal, 10*(3), 243–265.

Lakonishok, J., Shleifer, A., & Vishny, R. W. (1994, December). Contrarian investment, extrapolation, and risk. *The Journal of Finance, 49*(5), 1541–1578.

McLean, D., & Pontiff, J. (2014). Does academic research destroy stock return predictability? (Working Paper).

Odean, T. (1998, October). Are investors reluctant to realize their losses? *The Journal of Finance, 53*(5), 1775–1798.

Park, J., Konana, P., Gui, B., Kumar, A., & Raghunathan, R. (2010). Confirmation bias, overconfidence, and investment performance: Evidence from stock message boards. (Working Paper).

Patterson, S. (2010). *The quants.* Crown Publishing Group.

Patterson, S. (2012). *Dark pools: The rise of the machine traders and the rigging of the U.S. stock market.* Crown Publishing Group.

Piotroski, J. D. (2000). Value investing: The use of historical financial statement information to separate winners from losers. *Journal of Accounting Research, 38*[Supplement], 1–41.

Saunders, E. M., Jr. (1993). Stock prices and Wall Street weather. *The American Economic Review, 83*(5), 1337–1345.

Sensoy, B. A. (2009, April). Performance evaluation and self-designated benchmark indexes in the mutual fund industry. *Journal of Financial Economics, 92*(1), 25–39.

Zhang, L. (2005, February). The value premium. *The Journal of Finance, 60*(1), 67–103.

Index

financial journals

    finding ideas for new screens, 130-133

    regression techniques, 132

finding academic finance articles, 133

Finviz, 164

fool.com, 164

fore-knowledge, 70

fragility, technical analysis, 77-81

Franklin, Benjamin, 179

free trials of Equities Lab, 15

French, Kenneth, 175

frequency, rebalancing, 105

F-score, 114-116

full-service brokers, 152-153

fundamental fund, integrating with, 62

fundamental valuation

    case study: screener to help selection for deep analysis, 59-62

    cautions, 63

    overview, 59

fundamental valuation case study: integrating with fundamental fund, 62

fundamental-based weights, 111

future shock, 129

G

goals, investing goals and associated screeners, 29-32

good enough value screens, 124-127

    backtests, 125-126

Google finance stock screener, 12

graphs, 132

Greenblatt, Joel, 29, 117

growth stocks, 29, 168

H

hedge funds, competing against, 176-177

helping dad case study, 59-62

history of quantitative investing, 173-175

holdings, limiting number of, 53-54

horizons, 3-4

    life choices, 9

    long time horizons, 9

    screens, 3-4

    transaction costs, 3

I-J-K

ideas for new screens

    sources, 133

    understanding articles in financial journals, 130-133

implementation, explained, 5-6

implementing strategies, 5

    brokerage accounts, 146-148

        discount brokerages, 151-152

        full-service brokers, 152-153

        Interactive Brokers, 151

        Motif Investing, 148-151

    first steps, 146

    making as much as backtests suggest, 154-156

improving investment outcomes

    helping dad case study, 59-62

    integrating with a fundamental fund case study, 62

industries, diversification, 54-57

information for stock deep dive, 12

information frequency, horizons, 3

initial beliefs are wrong, troubleshooting, 137-138

V

W-X-Y-Z